Intermediate SCAT Practice Tests

Three Full-Length Verbal and Quantitative Mock Tests with Detailed Answer Explanations

Anthem Press
An imprint of Wimbledon Publishing Company
www.anthempress.com

This edition first published in UK and USA 2021
by ANTHEM PRESS
75–76 Blackfriars Road, London SE1 8HA, UK
or PO Box 9779, London SW19 7ZG, UK

and

244 Madison Ave #116, New York, NY 10016, USA

© Accel Learning LLC www.accellearning.com 2021

All rights reserved. Without limiting the rights under copyright reserved above, no part of this publication may be reproduced, stored or introduced into a retrieval system, or transmitted, in any form or by any means (electronic, mechanical, photocopying, recording or otherwise), without the prior written permission of both the copyright owner and the above publisher of this book.

British Library Cataloguing-in-Publication Data

A catalogue record for this book is available from the British Library.

Library of Congress Cataloging-in-Publication Data

A catalog record for this book has been requested.

ISBN-13: 978-1-83998-168-5 (Pbk)
ISBN-10: 1-83998-168-7 (Pbk)

This title is also available as an e-book.

Contents

Introduction iv

Practice Test 1 1
    Verbal Practice Test 2
    Quantitative Practice Test 15
    Answer Key 29
    Answer Key with Explanations 30

Practice Test 2 41
    Verbal Practice Test 42
    Quantitative Practice Test 55
    Answer Key 67
    Answer Key with Explanations 68

Practice Test 3 79
    Verbal Practice Test 80
    Quantitative Practice Test 93
    Answer Key 107
    Answer Key with Explanations 108

Introduction

The School and College Ability Test (SCAT) is a multiple-choice, standardized test administered by the Johns Hopkins Center for Talented Youth (CTY), a gifted education program for school-age children in the second to twelfth grades. It is an above-grade level test that assesses math and verbal reasoning abilities among gifted children and assesses students at a higher grade level than the one they are in at the time the test is administered.

Check here for more information about the CTY program: https://cty.jhu.edu/

There are three levels of SCAT:

1. Elementary Level SCAT – Students in grades 2–3 take the Elementary SCAT designed for students in grades 4–5.
2. Intermediate Level SCAT – Students in grades 4–5 take the Intermediate SCAT designed for students in grades 6–8.
3. Advanced Level SCAT - Students in grades 6 and above take the Advanced SCAT designed for students in grades 9–12.

The two sections for testing math and verbal reasoning are each 22-minutes long separated by a 10-minutes break. There are 55 multiple-choice questions per section, 5 of which are experimental.

The verbal section assesses the student's understanding of word definitions and consists of verbal reasoning analogy questions. In each question, students are presented with a pair of words that are related to each other in some way. They are then to select from the answer options a pair of words that shares the same relation.

The quantitative section assesses how well the student is able to work with numbers and consists of multiple-choice mathematical comparisons. Each question displays two quantities, of which the student needs to choose the one with the greater value.

Students are required to register with CTY to obtain an eligibility number before they can register to test at a Prometric test center. After receiving the eligibility number, students can book their SCAT test at the nearest Prometric test center by logging into their MyCTY account online here: https://cty.jhu.edu/talent/eligibility/index.html

Results of above-grade level assessments may confer the following eligibility levels:

- Advanced CTY Level: test scores that reflect ability approximately four grade levels above the current enrolled grade.
- CTY Level: test scores that reflect ability approximately two grade levels above the current enrolled grade.

Students may take the SCAT two times during any single academic year.

Students can view their results after taking the test on the John Hopkins MyCTY page here: https://mycty.jhu.edu/mycty2/login.cfm.

SCAT Scaled Scores are based on the number of questions the student answers correctly out of the 50 scored questions in each section. They range from 401 to 514 depending on the level the student takes as shown below:

- Elementary Level
  - Verbal Range = 401-471
  - Quantitative Range = 412-475
- Intermediate Level
  - Verbal Range = 405-482
  - Quantitative Range = 419-506
- Advanced Level
  - Verbal Range = 410-494
  - Quantitative Range = 424-514

Introduction

SCAT percentiles are used to compare students to the older population to whom the student will be compared. For example, Grade 2 students are compared to a general population of 4th graders and so on, as detailed below:

- Grade 2 is compared to Grade 4
- Grade 3 to Grade 5
- Grade 4 to Grade 6
- Grade 5 to Grade 8
- Grade 6 to Grade 9
- Grade 7 to Grade 12
- Grade 8 to Grade 12

Help your child in preparing for the SCAT test with these full-length practice tests

Practice Test 1

Verbal Practice Test

Directions:

Each question begins with two words. These two words go together in a certain way. Under them, there are four other pairs of words lettered A, B, C, and D.

Find the lettered pair of words that go together in the same way as the first pair of words.

1 farmer: plough

    A. doctor: heal

    B. carpenter: harrow

    C. teacher: school

    D. tailor: needle

Answer:

2 furniture: wood

    A. paper: smooth

    B. linen: flax

    C. fabric: cloth

    D. jewelry: glass

Answer:

3 hovel: dirty

    A. hub: busy

    B. shovel: land

    C. vacant: occupied

    D. damage: equip

Answer:

Grades 4–5　　　　　　　　　　　　　　　　　Practice Test 1 Session 1

4 miserly: cheap
- A. extravagant: unpleasant
- B. friendly: funny
- C. rapid: slow
- D. homogeneous: alike

Answer:

5 bristly: coarse
- A. synthetic: artificial
- B. scarcity: abundance
- C. gentle: blunt
- D. mend: damage

Answer:

6 mend: sewing
- A. edit: manuscript
- B. bet: gamble
- C. partition: divide
- D. fix: repair

Answer:

7 piercing: siren
- A. hushed: whisper
- B. crystal: jewel
- C. unlock: key
- D. dancing: feet

Answer:

8 sincere: honest
- A. entertaining: boring
- B. gained: retrieved
- C. extensive: pleasant
- D. gossiped: shout

Answer:

9 straight: crooked

    A. fantastic: splendid

    B. value: worth

    C. massive: passive

    D. optimist: pessimist

Answer:

10 defeat: victory

    A. cheerful: helpful

    B. clear: vague

    C. clever: smart

    D. game: contest

Answer:

11 hero: courage

    A. gymnast: flexible

    B. scary: afraid

    C. soldier: weak

    D. student: lovable

Answer:

12 scalpel: surgeon

    A. chief: army

    B. hospital: doctor

    C. food: chef

    D. sword: warrior

Answer:

13 trembling: fear

    A. thrilled: horror

    B. yawning: sleepy

    C. laughing: giggle

    D. singing: happy

Answer:

Grades 4–5   Practice Test 1 Session 1

14 engagement: marriage

    A. autumn: winter

    B. write: compose

    C. November: March

    D. wedding: couple

Answer:

15 dispute: arbiter

    A. conference: speaker

    B. poll: contestant

    C. trial: jury

    D. teach: teacher

Answer:

16 overspend: broke

    A. idea: notion

    B. sink: drown

    C. chaos: hostile

    D. save: prosperous

Answer:

17 cigarette: detrimental

    A. apple: helpful

    B. book: knowledge

    C. alcohol: dizziness

    D. food: hunger

Answer:

18 computer: hard disk

    A. dictionary: book

    B. bicycle: pedal

    C. fabric: yarn

    D. cart: engine

Answer:

Grades 4–5 Practice Test 1 Session 1

19 scallop: mollusk

    A. shallot: onion

    B. trade: goods

    C. debt: money

    D. snake: mammal

Answer:

20 top: spinning

    A. documentary: show

    B. clothespin: hang

    C. earth: rotation

    D. sun: expanding

Answer:

21 lizard: turtle

    A. shark: snake

    B. frog: mosquito

    C. salamander: bats

    D. frog: salamander

Answer:

22 gangster: crime

    A. policeman: protection

    B. monarch: royal

    C. priest: preach

    D. huckster: advertising

Answer:

23 Botany: plants

    A. Physiology: mind

    B. Virology: disease

    C. Ology: animals

    D. Astrology: Planets

Answer:

24 elephant: trumpet

    A. rain: patter

    B. bee: bray

    C. drum: loud

    D. thunder: cackle

Answer:

25 cobbler: shoes

    A. career: artist

    B. goldsmith: ornaments

    C. miner: gold

    D. producer: play

Answer:

26 sculptor: chisel

    A. blacksmith: anvil

    B. hairdresser: hair

    C. soldier: plumb

    D. mason: axe

Answer:

27 car: steering

    A. sketch: painting

    B. wallet: cash

    C. telephone: communicating

    D. cart: wheel

Answer:

28 servant: house

    A. gambler: court

    B. astronomer: planet

    C. engineer: factory

    D. umpire: pitch

Answer:

Grades 4–5 Practice Test 1 Session 1

29 area: hectare

　A. mass: weight

　B. work: power

　C. pressure: Pascal

　D. temperature: cold

Answer:

30 smash: badminton

　A. diamond: baseball

　B. ring: basketball

　C. ice: hockey

　D. dribble: volleyball

Answer:

31 dolorous: weepy

　A. courageous: coward

　B. sonorous: loud

　C. woozy: sleepy

　D. curious: smart

Answer:

32 paddy: rice

　A. bed: oyster

　B. bread: sandwich

　C. scene: play

　D. mountain: hill

Answer:

33 epilogue: novel

　A. dessert: meal

　B. party: celebration

　C. story: chapter

　D. drinks: beverage

Answer:

Grades 4–5 Practice Test 1 Session 1

34 escalator: people

  A. elevator: building
  B. carousel: luggage
  C. vehicle: passenger
  D. boat: swimmer

Answer:

35 break: shift

  A. minute: hour
  B. tradition: culture
  C. shield: sword
  D. artistic: idealistic

Answer:

36 death: scarcity

  A. birth: population
  B. knowledge: smart
  C. improving: hopeful
  D. substitute: replace

Answer:

37 contamination: food

  A. infection: body
  B. injection: medicine
  C. transportation: airplane
  D. evolution: man

Answer:

38 burglar: house

  A. pirate: ship
  B. doctor: hospital
  C. soldier: battlefield
  D. sailor: sailboat

Answer:

39 master: mistress

    A. rooster: chicken

    B. royal: king

    C. queen: princess

    D. gander: goose

Answer:

40 monk: monastery

    A. prince: mansion

    B. convict: prison

    C. soldier: asylum

    D. gypsy: burrow

Answer:

41 abandon: leave

    A. endless: limited

    B. kind: benevolent

    C. argument: agreement

    D. childish: attention

Answer:

42 flowers: bouquet

    A. chicken: brood

    B. sailors: ship

    C. soldiers: colony

    D. people: ministers

Answer:

43 moist: drench

    A. famous: renowned

    B. anger: shout

    C. quarrel: misunderstanding

    D. battle: war

Answer:

44 defeat: vanquish

    A. search: ransack

    B. destroy: terrible

    C. hopeful: pessimistic

    D. faded: brilliance

Answer:

45 hangar: airplane

    A. oil: engine

    B. garage: automobile

    C. highway: ramp

    D. classroom: board

Answer:

46 irrelevant: significance

    A. faded: brilliance

    B. blender: appliance

    C. stare: glance

    D. disagreement: acceptance

Answer:

47 holster: pistol

    A. club: rifle

    B. sheath: knife

    C. weapon: gun

    D. telescope: star

Answer:

48 candle: illuminate

    A. wick: light

    B. wind: breeze

    C. refrigerator: cool

    D. artifact: ancient

Answer:

Grades 4–5 Practice Test 1 Session 1

49 documentary: reality
  A. fop: appearance
  B. movie: artist
  C. troubled: danger
  D. career: fulfilment

Answer:

50 dictionary: definition
  A. book: paper
  B. atlas: map
  C. south: direction
  D. globe: longitude

Answer:

51 ransom: captive
  A. gratuity: service
  B. prisoner: freedom
  C. fight: military
  D. food: restaurant

Answer:

52 aglet: shoelace
  A. cash: money
  B. head: hairclip
  C. sting: stab
  D. island: archipelago

Answer:

53 often: seldom
  A. denial: reaction
  B. disease: curable
  C. obsolete: current
  D. anger: rage

Answer:

54 racket: tennis

    A. mallet: croquet

    B. net: ball

    C. court: boxing

    D. track: skating

Answer:

55 rapier: sword

    A. despot: ruler

    B. faith: religion

    C. safety: peril

    D. bone: skeleton

Answer:

Optional Break

Quantitative Practice Test

Directions:

Each question given below has two parts. One part is column A, the other part is column B. You must find out if one part is greater than the other, or if the parts are equal, you will choose one answer.

A. If the part in column A is greater

B. If the part in column B is greater

C. The two parts are equal

Question 1

Column A	Column B
The total cost of 4 shirts that cost $10 each.	The total cost of 5 shirts that cost $8 each.

Answer:

Question 2

Column A	Column B
$20(3x - 4)$	$60x + 80$

Answer:

Question 3

Column A	Column B
The sum of the even numbers from 1 to 10.	The sum of the odd numbers from 1 to 10.

Answer:

Grades 4–5 Practice Test 1 Session 2

Question 4

Column A	Column B
$(5 + 7) \times 3 - 6$	30

Answer:

Question 5

Column A	Column B
$\frac{5}{6} \times \frac{2}{5}$	$\frac{3}{4} \times \frac{4}{9}$

Answer:

Question 6

Column A	Column B
The perimeter of a rectangle whose length is 8 cm and the width is 6 cm.	The perimeter of a square whose side is 5 cm.

Answer:

Question 7

Column A	Column B
Largest positive factor 24	Smallest positive multiple of 24

Answer:

Question 8

Column A	Column B
The total cost of a pen for $1 and 2 books for $3	The total cost of a pen for $1 and 2 books for $3 each

Answer:

Question 9

Column A	Column B
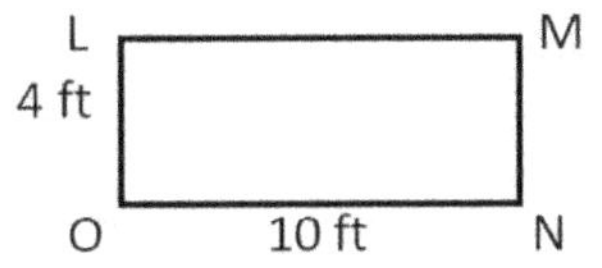 Perimeter of rectangle LMNO	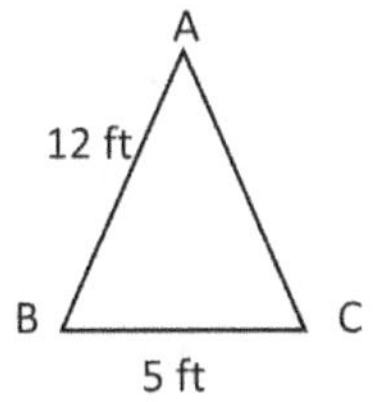 Perimeter of triangle ABC

Answer:

Question 10

Column A	Column B
25 × 4	20 + 20 + 20 + 20 + 20

Answer:

Question 11

Column A	Column B
50% of 1000	25% of 2000

Answer:

Question 12

Set A: {3, 4, 10, 12, 16}

Set B: {2, 5, 9, 11, 13, 17}

Column A	Column B
Median of Set A	Median of Set B

Answer:

Grades 4–5   Practice Test 1 Session 2

Question 13

Column A	Column B
Four times seven plus eight	The sum of five and three times four

Answer:

Question 14

Column A	Column B
GCF of 24 and 60	GCF of 50 and 70

Answer:

Question 15

A 6-sided number die, numbered 1 to 6, is rolled.

Column A	Column B
$\frac{2}{6}$	Probability that the number rolled is prime.

Answer:

Question 16

Column A	Column B
Area of a triangle whose base is 25 cm and height is 12 cm	Area of a square whose side is 7 cm long

Answer:

Question 17

Column A	Column B
The number of days in a week	The number of fingers in both hands

Answer:

Question 18

Column A	Column B
The mean of 6, 7, 10, and 13	The median of 6, 7, 10, and 13

Answer:

Question 19

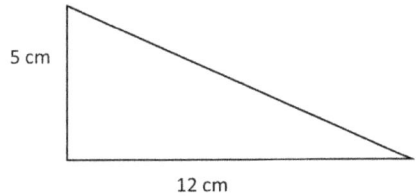

Column A	Column B
Area of the triangle	30 cm²

Answer:

Question 20

Column A	Column B
The common ratio of the sequence 1000, 500, 250, 125	The common ratio of the sequence 3, −6, 12, −24, 48

Answer:

Question 21

Column A	Column B
The remainder of 50 ÷ 7	The remainder of 70 ÷ 9

Answer:

Grades 4–5   Practice Test 1 Session 2

Question 22

3 triangles

4 squares

6 circles

8 hearts

Column A	Column B
The ratio of triangles to circles	The ratio of squares to hearts

Answer:

Question 23

Barbie has a small plot in the garden. She used $\frac{2}{5}$ of it to plant radishes and $\frac{2}{3}$ of it to plant carrots.

Column A	Column B
The part of the plot that she used to plant radishes	The part of the plot that she used to plant carrots

Answer:

Question 24

Column A	Column B
The dividend of a division sentence whose quotient is 68 and the divisor is 9	The dividend of a division sentence whose quotient is 12 and the divisor is 13

Answer:

Question 25

$\frac{2}{12}, \frac{4}{12}, \frac{3}{12}$

Column A	Column B
The sum of the fractions	The average of the fractions

Answer:

Question 26

Column A	Column B
The smallest prime number within the range of 20 to 30	23

Answer:

Question 27

Column A	Column B
(4 × 5 + 3) − 25 ÷ 5	4 × (5 + 3) − 25 ÷ 5

Answer:

Question 28

Column A	Column B
The LCM of 20 and 6	The LCD of $\frac{5}{20}$ and $\frac{3}{6}$

Answer:

Question 29

Column A	Column B
The product of seven and twelve divided by four	The product of seven and twelve minus four

Answer:

Question 30

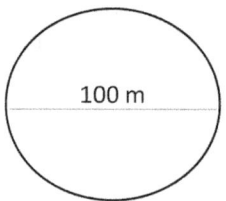

Column A	Column B
The diameter of the circle	The radius of the circle

Answer:

Question 31

Column A	Column B
75% of 30	30% of 75

Answer:

Question 32

Column A	Column B
Area of a circle with 5 cm radius	100

Answer:

Question 33

Column A	Column B
5.1	5.014

Answer:

Question 34

x > 0

Column A	Column B
4x	$\dfrac{x}{12}$

Answer:

Question 35

Column A	Column B
$5^2 + 5^2 + 5^2$	5^6

Answer:

Question 36

Column A	Column B
The lowest term of $\dfrac{8}{72}$	The lowest term of $\dfrac{2}{18}$

Answer:

Question 37

Column A	Column B
The total cost of 7 chocolates that cost $3 each and 4 chips that cost $2 each	The total cost of 8 chocolates that cost $7 each

Answer:

Grades 4–5 Practice Test 1 Session 2

Question 38

Lesley volunteered from 9:30 A.M. until 12:35 P.M.

Miya volunteered from 9:15 A.M. until 12:30 P.M.

Column A	Column B
The amount of time Lesley volunteered	The amount of time Miya volunteered

Answer:

Question 39

Column A	Column B
$2(3+5)^2 + 12$	$2 + (3+5)^2 + 12$

Answer:

Question 40

Column A	Column B
$\frac{3}{6} \times \frac{3}{5}$	$\frac{3}{6} \div \frac{5}{3}$

Answer:

Question 41

12, 20, 8, 14, 6

Column A	Column B
The sum of the integers	The average of the integers

Answer:

Question 42

Roger has 100 baseball cards. $\frac{1}{4}$ of them are new.

Column A	Column B
The number of new cards	The number of old cards

Answer:

Question 43

```
       4 ft
              25 ft
```

Column A	Column B
Half of the area of the rectangle	50 feet squared

Answer:

Question 44

Column A	Column B
The GCF of 15 and 60	The GCF of 20 and 40

Answer:

Question 45

y = 35

Column A	Column B
4y − 25	4(25) - y

Answer:

Grades 4–5   Practice Test 1 Session 2

Question 46

Column A	Column B
The value of 5 in 15,028	The value of 5 in 123,590

Answer:

Question 47

Column A	Column B
7 is added to the quotient of 27 and 3	7 is added to the product of 27 and 3

Answer:

Question 48

Karina printed 445 tickets for the school play on December. $\frac{3}{5}$ of the tickets were sold out last month.

Column A	Column B
The number of tickets that were sold last month	The number of tickets that remain to be sold

Answer:

Question 49

Column A	Column B
The number of sides that a pentagon has	The number of sides that a heptagon has

Answer:

Question 50

The price of a pair of shoes is $200. The price is then reduced by 20%.

Column A	Column B
$175	The final price of the pair of shoes after the reduction

Answer:

Grades 4–5   Practice Test 1 Session 2

Question 51

Column A	Column B
Volume of a rectangular solid whose length is 9 inches, width is 4 inches and height is 7 inches	Volume of a cube whose side is 7 inches

Answer:

Question 52

A 6-sided number die, numbered 1 to 6 is rolled.

Column A	Column B
The probability of getting a 4	$\frac{5}{6}$

Answer:

Question 53

Column A	Column B
The difference between 12,234 and 345	The difference between 12,342 and 354

Answer:

Question 54

Column A	Column B
Square of 81	Square root of 81

Answer:

Question 55

Ecia has $425.

Column A	Column B
Ecia's money after buying 8 notebooks that costs $3 each	Ecia's money after buying 5 notebooks that costs $7 each

Answer:

Answer Key

Verbal

#	Ans	#	Ans
1	D	29	C
2	B	30	A
3	A	31	B
4	D	32	A
5	A	33	A
6	A	34	B
7	A	35	A
8	B	36	D
9	D	37	A
10	B	38	A
11	A	39	D
12	D	40	B
13	B	41	B
14	A	42	A
15	C	43	A
16	D	44	A
17	A	45	B
18	B	46	A
19	A	47	B
20	C	48	C
21	D	49	A
22	D	50	B
23	D	51	A
24	A	52	D
25	B	53	C
26	A	54	A
27	D	55	A
28	D		

Quantitative

#	Ans	#	Ans
1	C	29	B
2	B	30	A
3	A	31	C
4	C	32	B
5	C	33	A
6	A	34	A
7	C	35	B
8	B	36	C
9	B	37	B
10	C	38	B
11	C	39	A
12	C	40	C
13	A	41	A
14	A	42	B
15	B	43	C
16	A	44	B
17	B	45	A
18	A	46	A
19	C	47	B
20	A	48	A
21	B	49	B
22	C	50	A
23	B	51	B
24	A	52	B
25	A	53	B
26	C	54	A
27	B	55	A
28	C		

Answer Key with Explanations

Verbal

1. **Answer:** D
   Explanation: Plough is a tool used by a farmer and needle is a tool used by a tailor.

2. **Answer:** B
   Explanation: Furniture is made of wood and linen is made of flax.

3. **Answer:** A
   Explanation: A hovel is described as dirty, while a hub is described as busy.

4. **Answer:** D
   Explanation: Miserly is another word for cheap and homogeneous is another word for alike.

5. **Answer:** A
   Explanation: Bristly is a synonym of coarse, while synthetic is a synonym of artificial.

6. **Answer:** A
   Explanation: One fixes sewing by mending, while one fixes manuscript by editing.

7. **Answer:** A
   Explanation: A siren is described as piercing and a whisper is described as hushed.

8. **Answer:** B
   Explanation: Someone who is sincere is honest and something that is gained is retrieved.

9. **Answer:** D
   Explanation: Straight is the opposite of crooked, while optimist is the opposite of pessimist.

10. **Answer:** B
    Explanation: The opposite of defeat is victory and the opposite of clear is vague.

11. **Answer:** A
    Explanation: A characteristic of a hero is to be full of courage and a characteristic of a gymnast is to be flexible.

12. **Answer:** D
    Explanation: A scalpel is a tool used by a surgeon and a sword is a tool used by a warrior.

13. **Answer:** B
    Explanation: Trembling is a sign of fear as yawning is a sign of being sleepy.

14. **Answer:** A
    Explanation: An engagement comes before marriage and autumn comes before winter.

15. **Answer:** C
    Explanation: An arbiter settles the dispute, while a jury settles the trial.

16	**Answer:** D

Explanation: Overspending results in being broke and saving results in a prosperous life.

17	**Answer:** A

Explanation: A cigarette is detrimental meaning unhelpful to someone's health, while an apple is helpful to someone's health.

18	**Answer:** B

Explanation: A hard disk is part of a computer and a pedal is part of a bicycle.

19	**Answer:** A

Explanation: A scallop is a type of mollusk and a shallot is a type of onion.

20	**Answer:** C

Explanation: Spinning is the movement of the top, while rotation is the movement of the earth.

21	**Answer:** D

Explanation: The lizard and turtle are kinds of reptiles, while frog and salamander are kinds of amphibians.

22	**Answer:** D

Explanation: A gangster is the one who deals in crime and a huckster is the one who deals in advertising.

23	**Answer:** D

Explanation: Botany is the study of plants and astrology is the study of planets.

24	**Answer:** A

Explanation: Trumpet is the sound produced by an elephant and patter is the sound produced by rain.

25	**Answer:** B

Explanation: A cobbler makes shoes and a goldsmith makes ornaments.

26	**Answer:** A

Explanation: Chisel is a tool used by a sculptor as anvil is a tool used by a blacksmith.

27	**Answer:** D

Explanation: A steering is part of a car and a wheel is part of a cart.

28	**Answer:** D

Explanation: A servant works in a house as an umpire works in a pitch.

29	**Answer:** C

Explanation: Hectare is a unit of area, while Pascal is a unit of pressure.

30	**Answer:** A

Explanation: Smash is a term used in the game of badminton and diamond is a term used in the game of baseball.

31	**Answer:** B

Explanation: Something that is dolorous is weepy and something that is sonorous is loud.

32 Answer: A

Explanation: Rice grows in a paddy, while oyster grows in a bed of ocean.

33 Answer: A

Explanation: An epilogue comes at the end of a novel and a dessert comes at the end of a meal.

34 Answer: B

Explanation: An escalator is used to move people as a carousel is used to move luggage.

35 Answer: A

Explanation: A break is part of a shift, while a minute is part of an hour.

36 Answer: D

Explanation: Death is a synonym of scarcity and substitute is the synonym of replace.

37 Answer: A

Explanation: Food gets affected by contamination and body gets affected by infection.

38 Answer: A

Explanation: A house is robbed by a burglar and a ship is robbed by a pirate.

39 Answer: D

Explanation: Master is the male, while mistress is the female. Gander is the male, while goose is the female.

40 Answer: B

Explanation: A monk lives in a monastery and a convict lives in a prison.

41 Answer: B

Explanation: Abandon is a synonym of leave as kind is a synonym of benevolent.

42 Answer: A

Explanation: A bunch of flowers is called a bouquet, while a group of chicken is called a brood.

43 Answer: A

Explanation: Something that is moist is very drench and something that is famous is very renowned.

44 Answer: A

Explanation: To vanquish is to defeat thoroughly as to ransack is to search thoroughly.

45 Answer: B

Explanation: A hangar houses an airplane, while a garage houses an automobile.

46 Answer: A

Explanation: Something that is irrelevant lacks significance and something that is faded lacks brilliance.

47 Answer: B

Explanation: A holster holds a pistol and a sheath holds a knife.

48 Answer: C

Explanation: A candle illuminates when in use as a refrigerator cools when in use.

Grades 4–5   Practice Test 1 Session 2

49   Answer: A

Explanation: A documentary is concerned with reality and a fop is concerned with appearance.

50   Answer: B

Explanation: A dictionary contains definitions and an atlas contains maps.

51   Answer: A

Explanation: A ransom is money paid for a captive and a gratuity is money paid for a service.

52   Answer: D

Explanation: An aglet is part of a shoelace and an island is part of an archipelago.

53   Answer: C

Explanation: Often is the opposite of seldom as obsolete is the opposite of current.

54   Answer: A

Explanation: A racket is used to play tennis and a mallet is used to play croquet.

55   Answer: A

Explanation: A rapier is a type of sword and a despot is a type of ruler.

Quantitative

1   Answer: C

Explanation: Find the total cost in each of the column by multiplying the number of shirts and the cost of each shirt. In Column A, there are 4 shirts that is $10 each, so 4($10) = $40. In Column B, there are 5 shirts that is $8 each, so 5($8) = $40. The columns are equal, so the correct answer is C.

2   Answer: B

Explanation: To know the answer, simplify the expression in Column A first. Distribute the 20 in the expression $20(3x - 4)$ to get $60x - 80$. Substitute a value for x to solve each column. Let x = 3. In Column A, 60(3) – 80 = 180 – 80 = 100. In Column B, 60(3) + 80 = 180 + 80 = 260. 260 is greater than 100; therefore the correct answer is B.

3   Answer: A

Explanation: Even numbers are numbers that can be divided exactly by 2, so the even numbers from 1 to 10 are 2, 4, 6, 8 and 10. To find the sum, add them. 2 + 4 + 6 + 8 + 10 = 30, so Column A is equal to 30. Odd numbers are numbers that cannot be divided exactly by 2, so the odd numbers from 1 to 10 are 1, 3, 5, 7, and 9. To find the sum, add them also. 1 + 3 + 5 + 7 + 9 = 25, so Column B is equal to 25. 30 is greater than 25; therefore the correct answer is A.

4   Answer: C

Explanation: Apply the PEMDAS Rule to evaluate the expression in Column A. Work within the parentheses first: (5 + 7) × 3 – 6 = 12 × 3 – 6. There are no exponents, so the next step is to do the multiplication and division from left to right: 12 × 3 – 6 = 36 – 6. Finally, add and subtract from left to right: 36 – 6 = 30. Since Column A is equal to Column B, the correct answer is C.

5 **Answer: C**

Explanation: To multiply fractions, multiply the numerators across and the denominators across. Reduce the answer to lowest term. For Column A, $\frac{5}{6} \times \frac{2}{5} = \frac{5 \times 2}{6 \times 5} = \frac{10}{30}$ or $\frac{1}{3}$. For Column B, $\frac{3}{4} \times \frac{4}{9} = \frac{3 \times 4}{4 \times 9} = \frac{12}{36}$ or $\frac{1}{3}$. Column A is equal to Column B, so the correct answer is C.

6 **Answer: A**

Explanation: Perimeter is the distance around a two-dimensional shape. To find the value of Column A, find the perimeter of a rectangle using the formula P = 2L + 2W, where L is the length and W is the width. Substitute the values: P = 2(8 cm) + 2(6 cm) = 16 cm + 12 cm = 28 cm, so Column A is equal to 28 cm. For Column B, find the perimeter of a square using the formula P = S + S + S + S, where S is the side of a square. Substitute the value: P = 5 cm + 5 cm + 5 cm + 5 cm = 20 cm, so Column B is equal to 20 cm. 28 cm is greater than 20 cm; therefore the correct answer is A.

7 **Answer: C**

Explanation: Factors refer to the numbers that when multiplied together are equal to another number. The largest positive factor of 24 is 24, since 1 × 24 = 24. Column A is equal to 24. Then, multiples refer to the result of multiplying two numbers together. The smallest positive multiple of 24 is also 24, since 24 × 1 = 24. Column B is also 24. Since the columns are equal, the correct answer is C.

8 **Answer: B**

Explanation: Find the total cost in each of the columns. In Column A, there is a pen that costs $1 and there are 2 books that cost $3, so $1 + $3 = $4. In Column B, there is a pen that costs $1 and there are 2 books that cost $3 each, so $1 + 2($3) = $1 + $6 = $7. $7 is greater than $4; therefore the correct answer is B.

9 **Answer: B**

Explanation: Find the perimeter of each figure. To find the perimeter of the rectangle LMNO, use the formula P = 2L + 2W, where L is the length and W is the width. Substitute the values: P = 2(10 ft) + 2(4 ft) = 20 ft + 8 ft = 28 ft, so Column A is 28 ft. To find the perimeter of the triangle ABC, add all the sides or P = S + S + S, where S is the side. Since the triangle is an isosceles triangle, line AB and line AC are equal length. Substitute the values: P = 12 ft + 12 ft + 5 ft = 29 ft, so Column B is 29 ft. Column B is greater than Column A; therefore the correct answer is B.

10 **Answer: C**

Explanation: Perform the indicated operation in each column. In Column A, 25 × 4 = 100, so Column A is equal to 100. In Column B, 20 + 20 + 20 + 20 + 20 = 100, so Column B is 100 also. Since they are equal, the correct answer is C.

11 **Answer: C**

Explanation: Find the percentage in each of the columns. To find the percentage, convert the percent into decimal form, then multiply it to the quantity. For Column A, 50% is 0.50 in decimal form. Now, multiply it to the quantity: 1000 × 0.50 = 500, thus Column A is equal to 500. For Column B, 25% is 0.25 in decimal form. Now, multiply it to the quantity: 2000 × 0.25 = 500, thus Column B is equal to 500 also. Both columns are equal to 500, therefore the correct answer is C.

12 **Answer: C**

Explanation: Median is the middle of a sorted list of numbers. There are five numbers in Set A, the median is the middle number in the list which is 5, so Column A is equal to 5. There are six numbers in Set B. Since there is no middle number, look for the middle pair of numbers and find the half way between them by adding them together and dividing by 2. The middle pair of numbers are 9 and 11: 9 + 11 = 20 ÷ 2 = 10, so Column B is equal to 10 also. Columns A and B are equal, so the correct answer is C.

| Grades 4–5 | Practice Test 1 Session 2 |

13 **Answer:** A

Explanation: Translate the given verbal sentence to mathematical sentence and solve. In Column A, four times seven plus eight is 4 × 7 + 8, when solved it is equal to 36. In Column B, the sum of five and three times four is (5 + 3) × 4, when solved it is equal to 32. 36 is greater than 32, so the correct answer is A.

14 **Answer:** A

| 24 – 1, 2, 3, 4, 6, 8, **12**, 24 |
| 60 – 1, 2, 3, 4, 5, 6, 10, **12**, 15, 20, 30, 60 |

| 50 – 1, 2, 5, **10**, 25, 50 |
| 70 – 1, 2, 5, 7, **10**, 14, 35, 70 |

Explanation: GCF stands for the greatest common factor. It is the highest factor that the numbers have in common. Let us use the listing method to know the GCF of the numbers.

The GCF of 24 and 60 is 12, so Column A is equal to 12. The GCF of 50 and 70 is 10, so Column B is equal to 10. 12 is greater than 10; therefore the correct answer is A.

15 **Answer:** B

Explanation: Prime numbers are whole numbers that have only two factors, 1 and the number itself. From the 6-sided die, the prime numbers are 2, 3 and 5. Remember that the probability is equal to the number of events to happen over the total number of possible outcomes; thus the probability of rolling a prime a number is $\frac{3}{6}$. Column B is equal to $\frac{3}{6}$ which is greater than the Column A which is $\frac{2}{6}$; therefore B is the correct answer.

16 **Answer:** A

Explanation: Find the area of each figure. For Column A, you have to find the area of a triangle using the formula $A = \frac{1}{2} bh$, where b is the base and h is the height. Substitute the values: $A = \frac{1}{2}$ (25 cm) (12 cm) = $\frac{1}{2}$ (300 cm²) = 150 cm², so Column A is 150 cm². For Column B, you have to find the area of a square using the formula $A = s^2$, where s is the side. Substitute the value: A = (7cm)² = 49 cm², so Column B is 49 cm². Column A is greater than Column B, so A is the correct answer.

17 **Answer:** B

Explanation: There are seven days in a week, so Column A is equal to 7. There are ten fingers in both hands, so Column B is equal to 10. 10 is greater than 7; therefore the correct answer is B.

18 **Answer:** A

Explanation: Mean is the average of the numbers. To find the mean, add up all the numbers and divide by how many numbers there are. For Column A, you have to add the numbers and divide the sum by 4, since there are four numbers. 6 + 7 + 10 + 13 = 36 ÷ 4 = 9, so Column A is equal to 9. Then, median is the middle number in a list. There are four numbers in Column B, so instead of getting the middle number, you have to add the middle pair of numbers and divide by 2. The middle pair of numbers are 7 and 10. 7 + 10 = 17 ÷ 2 = 8.5, so Column B is equal to 8.5. 9 is greater than 8.5, so A is the correct answer.

19 **Answer:** C

Explanation: The formula in finding the area of a triangle is $A = \frac{1}{2} bh$, where b is the base and h is the height. Substitute the values: $A = \frac{1}{2}$ (12 cm) (5 cm) = $\frac{1}{2}$ (60 cm²) = 30 cm². The area is 30 cm² and it is the same as the value in Column B, so the correct answer is C.

20 Answer: A

Explanation: Find the common ratio of each sequence. To find the common ratio, divide the successive pair of terms in the sequence.

$1000 \div 500 = 2$
$500 \div 250 = 2$
$250 \div 125 = 2$

$-6 \div 3 = -2$
$12 \div -6 = -2$
$-24 \div 12 = -2$
$48 \div -24 = -2$

The common ratio of the sequence in Column A is 2, while the common ratio of the sequence in Column B is –2. Positive 2 is greater than negative 2, so the correct answer is A.

21 Answer: B

Explanation: Remainder is the leftover after the division process. To know the remainder in each of the column, just divide. In Column A, 50 ÷ 7 = 7 r. 1, so Column A is equal to 1. In Column B, 70 ÷ 9 = 7 r. 7, so Column B is equal to 7. The correct answer is B, since 7 is greater than 1.

22 Answer: C

Explanation: A ratio indicates how many times one number contains another. The symbol ":" is used to separate the values. In Column A, you have to give the ratio of triangles to circles. Since there are 3 triangles and 6 circles, the ratio is 3:6. You can also simplify ratio, so 3:6 is equal to 1:2. In Column B, you have to give the ratio of squares to hearts. Since there are 4 squares and 8 hearts, the ratio is 4:8. You can also simplify it, so 4:8 is equal to 1:2. Both columns are equal to 1:2, so the correct answer is C.

23 Answer: B

Explanation: To know the value in each of the column, you have to make the fractions similar. There are three steps to make them similar. First, find the LCD or the least common denominator. Second, divide the LCD by the denominator and times the numerator. Third, write the new fraction using your answer in the second step as your numerator over the LCD. The denominators are 5 and 3, so the LCD is 15. For Column A, the part of the plot that she used for the radishes is $\frac{2}{5}$: 15 ÷ 5 × 2 = 6; thus it is $\frac{6}{20}$. For Column B, the part of the plot that she used for the carrots is $\frac{2}{3}$: 15 ÷ 3 × 2 = 10; thus it is $\frac{10}{20}$. Column B is greater than Column A, so the correct answer is B.

24 Answer: A

Explanation: The dividend refers to the value that we have to divide. To find the dividend, multiply the quotient and the divisor. In Column A, the quotient is 68 and the divisor is 9: 68 × 9 = 612. So Column A is equal to 612. In Column B, the quotient is 12 and the divisor is 13: 12 × 13 = 156. So Column B is equal to 156. The correct answer is A, since 612 is greater than 156.

25 Answer: A

Explanation: Find the value in each of the column. In Column A, you have to get the sum of the fractions. Since the fractions are similar, just add the numerators and copy the denominator. $\frac{2}{12} + \frac{4}{12} + \frac{3}{12} = \frac{9}{12}$ or $\frac{3}{4}$, so Column A is equal to $\frac{3}{4}$. In Column B, you have to get the average of the fractions by adding the fractions and dividing the sum by the number of fractions there are. Since you already know the sum of the fractions, you can proceed to dividing the sum by the number of fractions there are which is 3. $\frac{3}{4} \div 3 = \frac{3}{4} \times \frac{1}{3} = \frac{3}{12}$ or $\frac{1}{4}$, so Column B is equal to $\frac{1}{4}$. The correct answer is A, since $\frac{3}{4}$ is greater than $\frac{1}{4}$.

Grades 4–5 · Practice Test 1 Session 2

26 Answer: C

Explanation: Prime number is a number whose only factor is 1 and the number itself. There are two prime numbers within the range of 20 to 30. They are the numbers 23 and 29, but since Column A is looking for the smallest number, it is 23. The correct answer is C because the two columns have the same value.

27 Answer: B

Explanation: Apply the PEMDAS Rule to evaluate the expressions in both columns. In Column A, work within the parentheses first: $(4 \times 5 + 3) - 25 \div 5 = 23 - 25 \div 5$. There are no exponents, so do the multiplication and division from left to right: $23 - 25 \div 5 = 23 - 5$. Lastly, add and subtract from left to right: $23 - 5 = 18$. Do the same process in Column B. Work within the parentheses first: $4 \times (5 + 3) - 25 \div 5 = 4 \times 8 - 25 \div 5$. There are no exponents, so do the multiplication and division from left to right: $4 \times 8 - 25 \div 5 = 32 - 5$. Lastly, add and subtract from left to right: $32 - 5 = 27$. 27 is greater than 18, so the correct answer is B.

28 Answer: C

Explanation: In Column A, you have to look for the LCM of 20 and 6. LCM stands for the least common multiple. It is the smallest multiple that the numbers have in common. To find the LCM of the numbers, you can use the listing method wherein you are just going to list down the multiples of the numbers and get the smallest number that they have in common.

LCM: | 20 – 20, 40, **60**, 80, 100 |
      | 6 – 6, 12, 18, 24, 30, 36, 42, 48, 54, **60** |

Therefore, the LCM of 20 and 6 is 60. In Column B, you have to look for the LCD of the fractions. LCD stands for the least common denominator. Finding the LCD is the same as finding the LCM of the numbers. So, if the LCM of the numbers is 60, their LCD is 60 also. The value of both columns is equal, so the correct answer is C.

29 Answer: B

Explanation: To find the value in each of the column, you have to translate the verbal sentences to mathematical sentences first, then perform the operations. In Column A, the mathematical sentence of the product of seven and twelve divided by four is $(7 \times 12) \div 4$. Solve: $(7 \times 12) \div 4 = 84 \div 4 = 21$, so Column A is equal to 21. In Column B, the mathematical sentence of the product of seven and twelve minus four is $(7 \times 12) - 4$. Solve: $(7 \times 12) - 4 = 84 - 4 = 80$, so Column B is equal to 80. 80 is greater than 21; thus the correct answer is B.

30 Answer: A

Explanation: The diameter refers to the distance that goes straight across the circle, through the center. Based on the given above, the 100 m is the diameter of the circle, so Column A is equal to 100. The radius refers to the distance from the center outwards or it is the half of the diameter. Since the diameter is 100 m, divide it by 2 to get the half of it: $100 \text{ m} \div 2 = 50 \text{ m}$. 100 is greater than 50, so the correct answer is A.

31 Answer: C

Explanation: The word "of" means to multiply. In Column A, find the 75% of 30 by changing the percentage to a decimal number before you multiply: $0.75 \times 30 = 22.5$. In Column B, change the percentage to a decimal number also before you multiply: $0.30 \times 75 = 22.5$. Both columns are equal to 22.5; therefore the answer is C.

32 Answer: B

Explanation: Area is the size of a surface. To find the area of the circle in Column A, you have to use the formula $A = \pi r^2$, where π is equal to 3.1416 and r is the radius. Substitute the values: $A = (3.1416)(5 \text{ cm})^2 = (3.1416)(25 \text{ cm}^2) = 78.54 \text{ cm}^2$. 100 is greater than 78.54; therefore the correct answer is B.

33 **Answer:** A

Explanation: Compare the quantities. Add two zeros to quantity A to compare it with quantity B, and since the first digit of the two quantities have the same value and place value, move to the next number to compare: 5.100 and 5.014. In Column A, the tenths digit is 1 and in Column B, the tenths digit is 0; therefore Column A is greater than Column B. The correct answer is A.

34 **Answer:** A

Explanation: Try a number greater than 1 to find which column is greater, then substitute it to each quantity. Let us try 24. For Column A: 4x = 4(24) = 96. For Column B: $\frac{24}{12}$ = 2. The correct answer is A because whenever a number greater than 1 is multiplied by 4, it will be greater than if that number is divided by 5.

35 **Answer:** B

Explanation: Column A can be written out as (5 × 5) + (5 × 5) + (5 × 5) = 25 + 25 + 25 = 75. Column B can be written out as 5 × 5 × 5 × 5 × 5 × 5 = 15,625. Column B is greater than Column A; thus the correct answer is B.

36 **Answer:** C

Explanation: Lowest term is the simplest form of fraction. To give the lowest term of fraction, find the greatest common factor of the numerator and the denominator, then divide. In Column A, the greatest common factor of 8 and 72 is 8. Divide: 8 ÷ 8 = 1; 72 ÷ 8 = 9, so Column A is $\frac{1}{9}$. In Column B, the greatest common factor of 2 and 18 is 2. Divide: 2 ÷ 2 = 1; 18 ÷ 2 = 9, so Column B is $\frac{1}{9}$. Column A and Column B are equal, so the correct answer is C.

37 **Answer:** B

Explanation: Find the total amount in each of the column. In Column A, there are 7 chocolates that cost $3 each and 4 chips that cost $2 each: (7 × $3) + (4 × $2) = $21 + $8 = $29. In Column B, there are 8 chocolates that cost $7 each: 8 × $7 = $56. $56 is greater than $29, so the correct answer is B.

38 **Answer:** B

Explanation: Find the amount of time that Lesley and Miya volunteered by subtracting the starting time from the ending time. For Column A, the starting time is 9:30 A.M. and the ending time is 12:35 P.M., subtract: 12:35 − 9:30 = 3:05, so the amount of time Lesley volunteered was 3 hours and 5 minutes. For Column B, the starting time is 9:15 A.M. and the ending time is 12:30 P.M., subtract: 12:30 − 9:15 = 3:15, so the amount of time Miya volunteered was 3 hours and 15 minutes. Column B is greater than Column A, so the correct answer is B.

39 **Answer:** A

Explanation: Apply the PEMDAS Rule to evaluate the expressions in both columns. In Column A, work within the parentheses first: 2 (3 + 5)² + 12 = 2 (8)² + 12. Next is the exponent: 2 (8)² + 12 = 2(64) + 12. After the exponent, do the multiplication and division from left to right: 2(64) + 12 = 128 + 12. Lastly, add and subtract from left to right: 128 + 12 = 140. Do the same process in Column B. Work within the parentheses first: 2 + (3 + 5)² + 12 = 2 + (8)² + 12. Next is the exponent: 2 + (8)² + 12 = 2 + 64 + 12. There is no multiplication or division involved, so add and subtract from left to right: 2 + 64 + 12 = 78. 140 is greater than 78, so the correct answer is A.

40 **Answer:** C

Explanation: Evaluate the fractions. To multiply the fractions in Column A, multiply the numerator by the numerator and multiply the denominator by the denominator: $\frac{3}{6} \times \frac{3}{5} = \frac{9}{30}$ or $\frac{3}{10}$. To divide the fractions in Column B, change the division sign to multiplication sign and give the reciprocal of the second fraction: $\frac{3}{6} \div \frac{5}{3}$ =: $\frac{3}{6} \times \frac{3}{5} = \frac{9}{30}$ or $\frac{3}{10}$. They have the same value; therefore the correct answer is C.

| Grades 4–5 | Practice Test 1 Session 2 |

41 **Answer: A**

Explanation: For Column A, add the integers: 12 + 20 + 8 + 15 + 6 = 60. For Column B, find the average by dividing sum of the integers by the number of integers there are: 60 ÷ 5 = 12. 60 is greater than 12, so the correct answer is A.

42 **Answer: B**

Explanation: Find the number of new and old cards. To find the number of cards in Column A, get the $\frac{1}{4}$ of 100. The word "of" means to multiply: $\frac{1}{4} \times 100 = 25$. Therefore, there are 25 cards in column A. To find the number of cards in Column B, subtract the number of new cards from the total number of cards: 100 − 25 = 75. Therefore, there are 75 cards in Column B. Column B is greater than Column A, so the correct answer is B.

43 **Answer: C**

Explanation: To find the half of the area of the rectangle, you have to solve for the area first using the formula A = l × w, then divide it by 2. Substitute the values: A = 25 ft × 4 ft = 100 ft². Divide by 2: 100 ft² ÷ 2 = 50 ft². The correct answer is C, since 50 ft² and 50 feet squared are just the same.

44 **Answer: B**

Explanation: GCF stands for the greatest common factor. Listing method is one of the ways to find the GCF of the numbers. This method refers to listing down the factors of the numbers.

15 – 1, 3, 5, **15**
60 – 1, 2, 3, 4, 5, 6, 10, 12, **15**

20 – 1, 2, 4, 5, 10, **20**
40 – 1, 2, 4, 5, 10, **20**, 40

The GCF of the numbers in Column A is 15. The GCF of the numbers in Column B is 20. The correct answer is B, since 20 is greater than 15.

45 **Answer: A**

Explanation: Evaluate the expressions by substituting the value of y. In Column A, 4y − 25 = 4(35) − 25 = 140 − 25 = 115. In Column B, 4(25) − 35 = 100 − 35 = 65. Column A is greater than Column B, so the correct answer is A.

46 **Answer: A**

Explanation: The place value of digit of 5 in Column A is thousands, so its value is 5,000. The place value of digit 5 in Column B is hundreds, so the value of digit 5 is 500. 5,000 is greater than 500, so the correct answer is A.

47 **Answer: B**

Explanation: Translate the verbal sentence to mathematical sentence, then solve. In Column A, you have to add 7 to the quotient of 27 and 3. Remember that quotient is the answer in division, so you have to divide 27 and 3: 7 + (27 ÷ 3) = 7 + 9 = 16. In Column B, you have to add 7 to the product of 27 and 3. Remember that product is the answer in multiplication, so you have to multiply 27 and 3: 7 + (27 3) = 7 + 81 = 88. 88 is greater than 16; thus the correct answer is B.

48 **Answer: A**

Explanation: In Column A, find the number of tickets that were sold last month by getting the $\frac{3}{5}$ of 445. Remember that the word "of" means to multiply: $\frac{3}{5} \times 445 = \frac{1335}{5} = 267$, so there were 267 tickets that were sold last month. In Column B, to find the number of tickets that remain to be sold, subtract the number of tickets that were sold last month from the total number of tickets: 445 − 267 = 178. The correct answer is A, since 267 is greater than 178.

49 **Answer: B**

   Explanation: Pentagon and heptagon are polygons. The correct answer is B because the pentagon is a five-sided polygon and the heptagon is a seven-sided polygon.

50 **Answer: A**

   Explanation: Find the final price of the pair of shoes after the reduction by getting the 20% of $200 and subtracting it from the original price of the shoes. The word "of" means to multiply and remember to change the percentage to a decimal number. 20% of 200 = 0.20 × $200 = $40. Now, subtract: $200 - $40 = $160. The correct answer is A, since $175 is greater than the final price of the pair of shoes after the reduction which is $160.

51 **Answer: B**

   Explanation: Volume refers to the three-dimensional space occupied by an object. For Column A, the formula used to find the volume of a rectangular prism is V = l × w × h. Substitute the values: V = 9 inches × 4 inches × 7 inches = 252 inches^3. For Column B, the formula used to find the volume of a cube is V = s^3. Substitute the value: V = (7 inches)^3 = 343 inches^3. The volume of the cube which is 343 inches^3 is greater than the volume of the rectangular prism which is 252 inches^3, so the correct answer is B.

52 **Answer: B**

   Explanation: Probability tells how likely an event to happen. The formula in finding the probability is the number of events to happen/the total number of possible outcomes. The number of events to happen is 1, since there is just one 4 on the die. Then, the number of possible outcomes is 6, since there are 6 numbers on the die. Therefore, the probability of getting a 4 is $\frac{1}{6}$. The correct answer is B because the value in Column B which is $\frac{5}{6}$ is greater than $\frac{1}{6}$.

53 **Answer: B**

   Explanation: The difference is the answer in subtraction. In Column A, subtract the 345 from 12,234: 12,234 − 345 = 11,889. In Column B, subtract the 354 from 12,342: 12,342 − 354 = 11,988. The correct answer is B because 11,988 is greater than 11,889.

54 **Answer: A**

   Explanation: Find the value in each of the column. In Column A, you have to square 81 which means you have to multiply 81 by itself: $(81)^2$ = 6,561. In Column B, you have to find the square root of 81 which means the number that when you multiply by itself is equal to 81: $\sqrt{81}$ = 9. Column A is greater than Column B, so the correct answer is A.

55 **Answer: A**

   Explanation: Find the amount of money left to Ecia in each of the column. In Column A, multiply the number of notebooks by the cost of each, then subtract from Ecia's money: 8 × $3 = $24; $425 - $24 = $401. Do the same process in Column B: 5 × $7 = $35; $425 - $35 = $390. Column A which is $401 is greater than Column B which is $390, so the correct answer is A.

Practice Test 2

Verbal Practice Test

Directions:

Each question begins with two words. These two words go together in a certain way. Under them, there are four other pairs of words lettered A, B, C, and D.

Find the lettered pair of words that go together in the same way as the first pair of words.

1 bird: aviary

    A. butterfly: insect

    B. hare: burrow

    C. whale: mammal

    D. king: monarch

Answer:

2 anger: rage

    A. theme: story

    B. parade: party

    C. speak: shout

    D. unhappy: frown

Answer:

3 architect: design

    A. mason: wall

    B. cobbler: ornaments

    C. poet: song

    D. tailor: thread

Answer:

4 scarcity: abundance

    A. idea: notion

    B. slim: skinny

    C. flaw: defect

    D. chaos: peace

Answer:

5 sedate: calm

    A. fame: obscurity

    B. ban: prohibition

    C. brief: lengthy

    D. cordial: hostile

Answer:

6 people: crowd

    A. sheep: shoal

    B. bees: mob

    C. termites: colony

    D. riders: gang

Answer:

7 slumber: sleep

    A. bog: marsh

    B. funeral: lonely

    C. son: nuclear

    D. cold: contagious

Answer:

8 stars: astronomy

    A. battles: history

    B. autumn: winter

    C. princess: fairytale

    D. eclipse: moon

Answer:

9 stanza: poem

    A. measure: kitchen

    B. sugar: pint

    C. volume: encyclopedia

    D. music: compose

Answer:

10 pharaoh: dynasty

    A. plane: transport

    B. king: master

    C. president: democracy

    D. judge: justice

Answer:

11 flutter: flap

    A. giggle: dance

    B. chatter: talk

    C. deplete: increase

    D. better: great

Answer:

12 urn: ashes

    A. wealth: rich

    B. treasure: jewel

    C. purse: money

    D. inheritance: mansion

Answer:

13 quarry: marble

    A. hive: honey

    B. note: melody

    C. shield: sword

    D. veins: circulate

Answer:

14 cord: telephone

    A. screen: television

    B. clock: cockpit

    C. friend: companion

    D. prism: glass

Answer:

15 faculty: teachers

    A. fleet: trucks

    B. vamp: shoe

    C. treaty: peace

    D. bank: dollar

Answer:

16 roam: walk

    A. letter: symbol

    B. path: maze

    C. babble: speak

    D. silent: gossip

Answer:

17 chant: recite

    A. hammer: hold

    B. improving: helpful

    C. pummel: hit

    D. sorrow: joy

Answer:

18 lawyer: court

    A. producer: stage

    B. poet: office

    C. beautician: site

    D. worker: factory

Answer:

19 crown: head

  A. attic: house

  B. stairs: up

  C. roots: tree

  D. blade: sword

Answer:

20 duck: waddle

  A. mouse: squeak

  B. donkey: trot

  C. swim: turtle

  D. bird: frisk

Answer:

21 deer: fawn

  A. cockroach: nymph

  B. owl: flit

  C. sheep: cub

  D. insect: caterpillar

Answer:

22 arts: museum

  A. farm: field

  B. garden: house

  C. flowers: soil

  D. fodder: silo

Answer:

23 ax: chopping

  A. hammer: building

  B. pestle: grinding

  C. book: telling

  D. sword: killing

Answer:

24 nanny: child

    A. infant: baby

    B. kangaroo: animal

    C. groom: horse

    D. stable: horse

Answer:

25 barn: livestock

    A. ship: wooden

    B. hotel: visit

    C. dog: cage

    D. hostel: travelers

Answer:

26 castle: moat

    A. glade: woods

    B. royalty: horse

    C. water: moss

    D. palace: princess

Answer:

27 blight: potato

    A. rot: sheep

    B. wool: lamb

    C. fold: blanket

    D. stratus: cloud

Answer:

28 nourish: growth

    A. hungry: food

    B. coddle: comfort

    C. murmur: sound

    D. sleep: tired

Answer:

| Grades 4–5 | Practice Test 2 Session 1 |

29 levee: flood

   A. river: drown

   B. rain: water

   C. helmet: injury

   D. problem: solution

Answer:

30 reimburse: expenses

   A. doctor: charges

   B. insurance: bond

   C. fee: payment

   D. foot: bill

Answer:

31 stern: boat

   A. lecture: warning

   B. scruff: neck

   C. ocean: ship

   D. room: hotel

Answer:

32 nurse: hospital

   A. bailiff: courtroom

   B. beard: razor

   C. fungus: morel

   D. mother: supermarket

Answer:

33 armor: combat

   A. thimble: sewing

   B. shield: sword

   C. needle: sewing

   D. technology: robot

Answer:

34 dome: stadium

   A. post: board

   B. harmony: cacophony

   C. canopy: bed

   D. scene: local

Answer:

35 cabana: pool

   A. balls: billiards

   B. tent: cabin

   C. plume: feather

   D. chalet: mountain

Answer:

36 mural: wall

   A. inscription: plaque

   B. caliber: bullet

   C. harvest: plant

   D. rational: proof

Answer:

37 puppies: furry

   A. medicine: delicious

   B. fish: slippery

   C. horse: donkey

   D. dinosaur: extinct

Answer:

38 sandpaper: rough

   A. career: professional

   B. artist: idealistic

   C. sunburn: heat

   D. carelessness: clumsy

Answer:

Grades 4–5　　　　　　　　　　　　　　　　　　　　　Practice Test 2 Session 1

39 bicycle: unicycle

    A. scarf: shawl

    B. wolves: wolf

    C. car: truck

    D. glasses: monocle

Answer:

40 pilgrim: journey

    A. world: explore

    B. recluse: home

    C. gullible: belief

    D. priest: evil

Answer:

41 queue: line

    A. stock: soup

    B. cinder: ash

    C. query: question

    D. stopper: cork

Answer:

42 crime: sin

    A. wish: desire

    B. refuse: renowned

    C. speak: anger

    D. moist: humid

Answer:

43 salt: seasoning

    A. parsley: garnish

    B. grain: wheat

    C. glucose: chocolate

    D. youth: child

Answer:

44 neck: guitar

   A. throw: pitch

   B. shaft: spear

   C. meal: drinks

   D. television: radio

Answer:

45 ruler: length

   A. inch: thumb

   B. meter stick: line

   C. protractor: angle

   D. T-square: weight

Answer:

46 phenomenon: phenomena

   A. event: celebration

   B. die: dice

   C. drab: bard

   D. hydrant: water

Answer:

47 parrot: mimic

   A. smile: fear

   B. horse: neigh

   C. chicken: brood

   D. dog: hound

Answer:

48 approve: sanction

   A. reprove: chide

   B. kiss: affection

   C. damage: repair

   D. improve: device

Answer:

49 turbine: engine

    A. turban: headdress

    B. urban: legend

    C. robe: wear

    D. robot: steel

Answer:

50 shield: armor

    A. bow: arrow

    B. gun: bullet

    C. equipment: gear

    D. knife: weapon

Answer:

51 shirt: trousers

    A. horse: carriage

    B. binocular: view

    C. cup: coffee

    D. chair: furniture

Answer:

52 nephew: niece

    A. brother: father

    B. horse: mare

    C. soldiers: army

    D. cousin: relative

Answer:

53 fish: aquarium

    A. birds: house

    B. mouse: scamper

    C. clothes: wardrobe

    D. owl: flit

Answer:

54 eskimo: igloo

    A. dentist: dental

    B. bear: iceberg

    C. peasant: cottage

    D. eagle: cage

Answer:

55 musicians: band

    A. cattle: herd

    B. ostrich: bird

    C. grains: granary

    D. car: garage

Optional Break

Quantitative Practice Test

Directions:

Each question given below has two parts. One part is column A, the other part is column B. You must find out if one part is greater than the other, or if the parts are equal, you will choose one answer.

A. If the part in column A is greater

B. If the part in column B is greater

C. The two parts are equal

Question 1

Column A	Column B
54% of 360	150

Answer:

Question 2

Column A	Column B
25 + (7 × 1.5) − 10	(25 + 7) × 1.5 − 10

Answer:

Question 3

Column A	Column B
The least prime number greater than 24	The least prime number less than 28

Answer:

Grades 4–5 Practice Test 2 Session 2

Question 4

$z > 1$

Column A	Column B
$7z - 5$	$2z + 5$

Answer:

Question 5

Column A	Column B
$(-3)^7$	$(-3)^6$

Answer:

Question 6

Column A	Column B
$a(b + c)$	$ab + ac$

Answer:

Question 7

Column A	Column B
$\frac{3}{6}$ of 12	$\frac{3}{5}$ of 20

Answer:

Question 8

Column A	Column B
Number of prime numbers between 4 and 20	5

Answer:

Question 9

1 < y < z > 1

Column A	Column B
y^2	z^2

Answer:

Question 10

Column A	Column B
Area of a square whose perimeter is 240 cm	Area of a rectangle whose length is 20 cm and width is 10 cm

Answer:

Question 11

Column A	Column B
The total cost of 3 pairs of shoes that cost $15 each	The total cost of 15 pairs of socks that cost $3 each

Answer:

Question 12

Column A	Column B
$\dfrac{89}{5}$	$\dfrac{90}{6}$

Answer:

Question 13

Column A	Column B
The number of years from 1621 to 1812	The number of years from 1631 to 1822

Answer:

Question 14

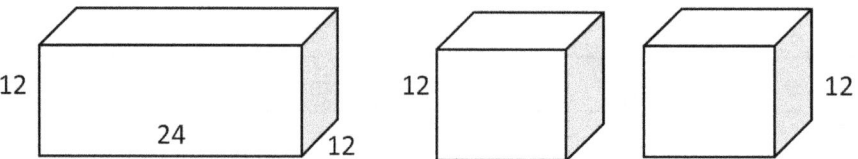

Note: Volume of a rectangular prism: V = l × w × h

Volume of a cube: V = s³

Column A	Column B
Volume of the rectangular prism	Total volume of the cubes

Answer:

Question 15

123,789

Column A	Column B
The value of 7	The value of 9

Answer:

Question 16

x > 5

Column A	Column B
$\dfrac{12x + 4}{5}$	$\dfrac{12x - 4}{5}$

Answer:

Question 17

Column A	Column B
6(m − 2n)	6m − 12n

Answer:

Question 18

Column A	Column B
$40 - $25	The total cost of 5 sachets of coffee for $3 each

Answer:

Question 19

Column A	Column B
The GCF of 15, 21, and 12	The GCF of 8, 30 and 42

Answer:

Question 20

Column A	Column B
The number of eights in 72	The number of nines in 72

Answer:

Question 21

Column A	Column B
The number of months in a year	The number of eggs in a dozen

Answer:

Question 22

Column A	Column B
5000 + 400 + 60 + 7 + 0.2 + .05	5,467.05

Answer:

Grades 4–5　　　　　　　　　　　　　　　　　　Practice Test 2 Session 2

Question 23

6, 20, 36

Column A	Column B
The LCM of the numbers	The sum of the numbers

Answer:

Question 24

Column A	Column B
10	$\sqrt{(65+56)}$

Answer:

Question 25

Column A	Column B
2^7	14

Answer:

Question 26

n = 46

Column A	Column B
The remainder when n is divided by 7	The remainder when n is divided by 5

Answer:

Question 27

The number of students in class C is 5 less than twice the number of students in class D. There are x students in class D.

Column A	Column B
The number of students in class C	2x – 5

Answer:

Question 28

1 meter = 100 centimeters

Column A	Column B
The perimeter of a square ground floor with sides of 4 meters	1,000 cm

Answer:

Question 29

Column A	Column B
1,225 more than 2,345	2,345 times 2

Answer:

Question 30

Column A	Column B
The total number of legs of 12 chickens	The total number of legs of 6 cows

Answer:

Question 31

Column A	Column B
One hundred thirty-six	One hundred thirty-seven thousandths

Answer:

Question 32

Column A	Column B
Twice an odd integer less than 6	Thrice an odd integer less than 9

Answer:

Question 33

1 kilogram = 1,000 grams

Column A	Column B
The total weight of three bags weighing 1.5 kilograms each	The total weight of two sacks weighing 2,000 grams each

Answer:

Question 34

Column A	Column B
The odd integer multiplied by 6 minus 7	The odd integer multiplied by 7 minus 6

Answer:

Question 35

Column A	Column B
The greatest prime factor of 36	The greatest prime factor of 48

Answer:

Question 36

Vexana is 5 years older than Odette.

Odette is 12 years old.

Column A	Column B
Vexana's present age	Odette's age in 3 years

Answer:

Question 37

Column A	Column B
40,000	$(201.70)^2$

Answer:

Question 38

A jar contains three different colors of marbles. There are 12 red, 7 blue and 10 green marbles.

Column A	Column B
The probability of picking a green marble	The probability of picking a blue marble

Answer:

Question 39

$A < C, B > D > 0$

Column A	Column B
A - B	C - D

Answer:

Question 40

A windmill makes one revolution every 15 seconds.

Column A	Column B
6	The number of revolutions made in 3 minutes

Answer:

Question 41

Column A	Column B
15 percent of 90	90 percent of 15

Answer:

Question 42

Column A	Column B
$\frac{4}{5} + \frac{4}{5}$	$1\frac{3}{5}$

Answer:

Question 43

Column A	Column B
The median of 12, 6, 7, 15 and 11	The mean of 12, 6, 7, 15 and 11

Answer:

Question 44

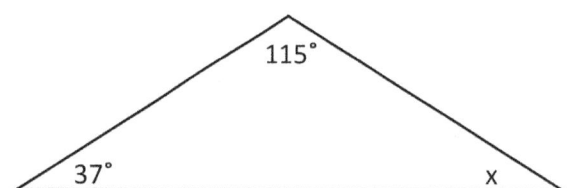

Column A	Column B
x	45°

Answer:

Question 45

Column A	Column B
75,356 rounded to the nearest hundreds	75,404 rounded to the nearest tens

Answer:

Question 46

$\frac{2}{7}, \frac{4}{7}, \frac{3}{7}, \frac{6}{7}$

Column A	Column B
The greatest fraction shown	The product of the smallest fraction and $\frac{3}{7}$

Answer:

Question 47

Column A	Column B
The number of hours from 6:30 P.M. to 10:45 P.M	4 hours and 30 minutes

Answer:

Question 48

Column A	Column B
The square root of 30	The greatest prime factor of 30

Answer:

Question 49

Column A	Column B
0.75 hour	45 minutes

Answer:

Question 50

Column A	Column B
The value of 5 in 234.785	5 hundredths

Answer:

Grades 4–5   Practice Test 2 Session 2

Question 51

Column A	Column B
(12 + 20) × 15 ÷ 3	(12 + 20) × (15 ÷ 3)

Answer:

Question 52

There are 150 people in a movie theater. 75 of the people are women, 60 people are men, and the remainder are children.

Column A	Column B
The number of children	50

Answer:

Question 53

Column A	Column B
16.5×10^5	0.165×10^7

Answer:

Question 54

The ratio of dogs to cats in a pet store is 5:3. There are 96 dogs and cats in the store.

Column A	Column B
The number of dogs in the pet store	65

Answer:

Question 55

Column A	Column B
5(4x + 6)	4(5x + 6)

Answer Key

Verbal

1. B
2. C
3. A
4. D
5. B
6. C
7. A
8. A
9. C
10. C
11. C
12. C
13. A
14. A
15. A
16. C
17. C
18. D
19. A
20. B
21. A
22. D
23. B
24. C
25. D
26. A
27. A
28. B
29. C
30. D
31. B
32. A
33. A
34. C
35. D
36. A
37. B
38. B
39. D
40. B
41. C
42. A
43. A
44. B
45. C
46. B
47. D
48. A
49. A
50. C
51. A
52. B
53. C
54. C
55. A

Quantitative

1. A
2. A
3. A
4. A
5. B
6. C
7. B
8. A
9. B
10. A
11. C
12. A
13. C
14. C
15. A
16. A
17. C
18. C
19. A
20. A
21. C
22. A
23. A
24. B
25. A
26. A
27. C
28. A
29. B
30. C
31. A
32. B
33. A
34. B
35. C
36. A
37. B
38. A
39. B
40. A
41. C
42. C
43. A
44. B
45. C
46. C
47. B
48. A
49. C
50. B
51. C
52. B
53. B
54. B
55. A

Answer Key with Explanations

Verbal

1. **Answer:** B
   Explanation: A bird lives in an aviary and a hare lives in a burrow.

2. **Answer:** C
   Explanation: Rage is of higher intensity than anger and shout is of higher intensity than speaking.

3. **Answer:** A
   Explanation: An architect makes a design as a mason constructs a wall.

4. **Answer:** D
   Explanation: Scarcity is the opposite of abundance, while chaos is the opposite of peace.

5. **Answer:** B
   Explanation: Sedate is a synonym of calm as ban is a synonym of prohibition.

6. **Answer:** C
   Explanation: A group of people is called crowd and a group of termites is called colony.

7. **Answer:** A
   Explanation: Slumber is a synonym of sleep and bog is a synonym of marsh.

8. **Answer:** A
   Explanation: Stars are part of astronomy and battles are part of history.

9. **Answer:** C
   Explanation: A stanza is part of a poem as a volume is part of an encyclopedia.

10. **Answer:** C
    Explanation: A pharaoh is the head of a dynasty and a president is the head of democracy.

11. **Answer:** C
    Explanation: To flutter is to flap rapidly and to chatter is to talk rapidly.

12. **Answer:** C
    Explanation: An urn is used to hold ashes as purse is used to hold money.

13. **Answer:** A
    Explanation: A quarry yields marble and a hive yields honey.

14. **Answer:** A
    Explanation: A cord is part of a telephone and a screen is part of a television.

15. **Answer:** A
    Explanation: A faculty is a group of teachers as fleet is a group of trucks.

Grades 4–5 Practice Test 2 Session 1

16 Answer: C

Explanation: Roam is a way to walk and babble is a way to speak.

17 Answer: C

Explanation: To chant is to recite repeatedly and to pummel is to hit repeatedly.

18 Answer: D

Explanation: A lawyer works in a court as a worker works in a factory.

19 Answer: A

Explanation: A crown is the upper part of the head and an attic is the upper part of a house.

20 Answer: B

Explanation: Waddle is the name given to the movement of a duck, while trot is the name given to the movement of a donkey.

21 Answer: A

Explanation: A fawn is the young one of a frog and a nymph is the young one of a cockroach.

22 Answer: D

Explanation: Arts are kept in a museum as fodder is kept in a silo.

23 Answer: B

Explanation: An ax is used for chopping and a pestle is used for grinding.

24 Answer: C

Explanation: A nanny takes care of a child, while a groom takes care of a horse.

25 Answer: D

Explanation: A barn is used as shelter for livestock and a hostel is used as shelter for travelers.

26 Answer: A

Explanation: A castle is surrounded by moat and a glade is surrounded by woods.

27 Answer: A

Explanation: A blight is a disease that strikes potatoes as a rot is a disease that strikes sheep.

28 Answer: B

Explanation: To nourish is to encourage growth and to coddle is to encourage comfort.

29 Answer: C

Explanation: A levee prevents flood and a helmet prevents injury.

30 Answer: D

Explanation: To reimburse means to pay expenses, while to foot means to pay a bill.

31 Answer: B

Explanation: A stern is the back of a boat as a scruff is the back of the neck.

32 **Answer:** A

Explanation: A nurse works in a hospital as a bailiff works in a courtroom.

33 **Answer:** A

Explanation: An armor is worn for protection in a combat and a thimble is worn for protection in sewing.

34 **Answer:** C

Explanation: A dome covers a stadium, while a canopy covers a bed.

35 **Answer:** D

Explanation: A cabana can be found near a pool and a chalet can be found near a mountain.

36 **Answer:** A

Explanation: A mural is painting that appears on a wall and an inscription appears on a plaque.

37 **Answer:** B

Explanation: A characteristic of a puppy is to be furry and a characteristic of a fish is to be slippery.

38 **Answer:** B

Explanation: A characteristic of a sandpaper is to be rough and a characteristic of an artist is to be idealistic.

39 **Answer:** D

Explanation: A unicycle has one wheel while a bicycle has two wheels. A monocle has one lens while glasses has two lens.

40 **Answer:** B

Explanation: A pilgrim can be found on a journey and a recluse can be found at home.

41 **Answer:** C

Explanation: A queue is another word for line and a query is another word for question.

42 **Answer:** A

Explanation: Sin is of higher intensity than crime and desire is of higher intensity than wish.

43 **Answer:** A

Explanation: Salt is used as a seasoning and parsley is used as a garnish.

44 **Answer:** B

Explanation: A neck is part of a guitar as a shaft is part of a spear.

45 **Answer:** C

Explanation: A ruler is used to measure length and a protractor is used to measure an angle.

46 **Answer:** B

Explanation: Phenomenon is the singular of phenomena and die is the singular of dice.

47 **Answer:** D

Explanation: To parrot means mimic and to dog means to hound.

| Grades 4–5 | Practice Test 2 Session 2 |

48 **Answer:** A

Explanation: Approve is a synonym of sanction and reprove is a synonym of chide.

49 **Answer:** A

Explanation: A turbine is a type of engine, while a turban is a type of headdress.

50 **Answer:** C

Explanation: A shield is a synonym of armor and an equipment is a synonym of gear.

51 **Answer:** A

Explanation: Shirt and trousers make pair, while horse and carriage make pair.

52 **Answer:** B

Explanation: A nephew is the male, while a niece is the female. A horse is the male, while a mare is the female.

53 **Answer:** C

Explanation: Fish are kept in an aquarium, while clothes are kept in a wardrobe.

54 **Answer:** C

Explanation: An eskimo lives in an igloo while a peasant lives in a cottage.

55 **Answer:** A

Explanation: A group of musicians is called a band as a group of cattle is called as a herd.

Quantitative

1 **Answer:** A

Explanation: Find the 54% of 360. Remember that the word "of" means to multiply and you have to make the percent to a decimal number: $0.54 \times 360 = 194.40$. The correct answer is A, since 194.40 is greater than 150.

2 **Answer:** A

Explanation: Apply the PEMDAS Rule to evaluate the expressions in both columns. In Column A, work within the parentheses first: $25 + (7 \times 1.5) - 10 = 25 + 10.5 - 10$. There are no exponents and multiplication and division, so add and subtract from left to right: $25 + 10.5 - 10 = 35.5 - 10 = 25.5$. Do the same process in Column B. Work within the parentheses first: $(25 + 7) \times 1.5 - 10 = 32 \times 1.5 - 10$. There is no exponent, so do the multiplication and division from left to right: $32 \times 1.5 - 10 = 48 - 10$. Now, add and subtract from left to right: $48 - 10 = 38$. 48 is greater than 38, so the correct answer is A.

3 **Answer:** A

Explanation: Prime numbers are numbers whose only factor is 1 and the number itself. In Column A, the least prime number greater than 24 is 29. In Column B, the least prime number less than 28 is 23. Column A is greater than Column B, so the correct answer is A.

4 **Answer:** A

Explanation: Plug in a value for z that is greater than 1. Let z be equal to 5. In Column A, $7z - 5 = 7(5) - 5 = 35 - 5 = 30$. In Column B, $2z + 5 = 2(5) + 5 = 10 + 5 = 15$. The correct answer is A, because whenever a number greater than 1 is plugged into the expressions, Column A will be always greater than Column B.

5 **Answer: B**

Explanation: Write out the expressions. In Column A, you have to multiply −3 seven times by itself and it can be written as −3 × −3 × −3 × −3 × −3 × −3 × −3 = −2,187. In Column B, you have to multiply −3 six times by itself and it can be written as −3 × −3 × −3 × −3 × −3 × −3 = 729. The correct answer is B, because a positive number is always greater than a negative number.

6 **Answer: C**

Explanation: In Column A, you have to distribute a in the expression a (b + c). You would get ab + ac. The correct answer is C, since both columns have the same expressions.

7 **Answer: B**

Explanation: The word "of" means to multiply. For Column A, find the $\frac{3}{6}$ of 12: $\frac{3}{6} \times 12 = \frac{36}{6} = 6$, so Column A is equal to 6. In Column B, find the $\frac{3}{5}$ of 20: $\frac{3}{5} \times 20 = \frac{60}{5} = 12$, so Column B is equal to 12. The correct answer is B, since 12 is greater than 6.

8 **Answer: A**

Explanation: Remember that prime numbers are numbers whose only factors are 1 and the number itself. In Column A, the prime numbers between 4 and 20 are 5, 7, 11, 13, 17 and 19, so there are 6 prime numbers. 6 is greater than 5, so the correct answer is A.

9 **Answer: B**

Explanation: Plug in a value for each variable. Notice that the value of variable y should be less than z, such that y is greater than 1. Then the value of variable z should be greater than y, such that z is greater than 1. Let y be equal to 4 and z equal to 5. In Column A, plug in the value of y which is 4: $y^2 = 4^2 = 16$. In Column B, plug in the value of z which is 5: $z^2 = 5^2 = 25$. The correct answer is B, since any value plugged into the variables considering the given condition of each value, Column B is always greater than Column A.

10 **Answer: A**

Explanation: Area is the size of a surface. In Column A, the formula to find the area of the square is $A = s^2$ where s is the side of the square. Considering the given perimeter of the square, you can find the measure of its side by dividing the perimeter by 4, since square has four sides: 240 cm ÷ 4 = 60 cm. Now solve for the area: $A = (60 \text{ cm})^2 = 3600 \text{ cm}^2$. In Column B, the formula to find the area of the rectangle is A = l × w where l is the length and w is the width: A = 20 cm × 10 cm = 200 cm². Column A is greater than Column A; thus the correct answer is A.

11 **Answer: C**

Explanation: Find the value in each of the column. In column A, multiply the number of pairs of shoes by the cost of each: 3 × $15 = $45. In column B, multiply the number of pairs of socks by the cost of each: 15 × $3 = $45. Both columns are equal to $45, so the correct answer is C.

12 **Answer: A**

Explanation: Simplify the fraction in each of the column. To simplify, divide the numerator by the denominator. In Column A, the fraction is $\frac{89}{5}$, so 89 divided by 5: 89 ÷ 5 = 17 r. 4 = $17\frac{4}{5}$. In Column B, the fraction is $\frac{90}{6}$, so 90 divided by 6: 90 ÷ 6 = 15. $17\frac{4}{5}$ is greater than 15; therefore the correct answer is A.

13 **Answer: C**

Explanation: Find the value in each of the column by subtracting the number of years. In Column A, subtract 1621 from 1812: 1812 − 1621 = 191. In Column B, subtract 1631 from 1822: 1822 − 1631 = 191. The correct answer is C, since Column A and Column B are equal.

| Grades 4–5 | Practice Test 2 Session 2 |

14 **Answer: C**

Explanation: Use the formula given to find the volume of the figures. In Column A, the length is 24 and the width and height are 12. Plug in the dimensions of the rectangular prism in the formula: V = 24 × 12 × 12 = 3,456. Column A is 3,456. In Column B, find the volume of each cube and then add the results together. Alternatively, since the two cubes have the same dimensions, just multiply the volume formula by 2 to find the total volume. Plug in the dimension of the cube: V = $2(12^3)$ = 2(1,728) = 3,456. The correct answer is C, since the columns are equal.

15 **Answer: A**

Explanation: Find the value of each digit in the given number. In Column A, the place value of 7 in 123,789 is hundreds, so its value is 700. Column A is 700. In Column B, the place value of 9 in 123,789 is ones, so its value is 9. Column B is 9. 700 is greater than 9, so the correct answer is A.

16 **Answer: A**

Explanation: Plug in a value for x. Notice that the value of x should be greater than 5. Let x be 6. Plug in the value in the expression in Column A: $\frac{12(6)+4}{5} = \frac{72+4}{5} = \frac{76}{5} = 15\frac{1}{5}$. Column A is $15\frac{1}{5}$. Plug in the value in the expression in Column B: $\frac{12(6)-4}{5} = \frac{12(6)-4}{5} = \frac{72-4}{5} = \frac{68}{5} = 13\frac{3}{5}$. Column B is $13\frac{3}{5}$. The correct answer is A, since Column A is greater than Column B.

17 **Answer: C**

Explanation: In Column A, distribute 6 in the expression 6(m – 2n). You would get 6m – 12n. The two columns are equal, so the correct answer is C.

18 **Answer: C**

Explanation: Find the value in each of the columns. In Column A, just perform the indicated operation: $40 - $25 = $15. Column A is $15. For Column B, multiply the number of sachets of coffee by the cost of each sachet: 5 × $3 = $15. Column A and Column B are equal, so the correct answer is C.

19 **Answer: A**

Explanation: GCF stands for the greatest common factor. It is the highest common factor that can be divided exactly into the numbers. Listing method is one of the ways to find the GCF of numbers. In listing method, you just have to list down the factors of every number.

| 15 – 1, 3, 5, 15 |
| 21 – 1, 3, 7, 21 |
| 12 – 1, 2, 3, 4, 6, 12 |

GCF: 3

| 8 – 1, 2, 4, 8 |
| 30 – 1, 2, 3, 5, 6, 10, 15, 30 |
| 42 – 1, 2, 3, 6, 7, 14, 21, 42 |

GCF: 2

In Column A, the GCF of the numbers is 3. In Column B, the GCF of the numbers is 2. 3 is greater than 2; thus the correct answer is A.

20 **Answer: A**

Explanation: Find the value in each of the column. In Column A, you have to know how many eights there are in 72. To do that, divide 72 by 8: 72 ÷ 8 = 9; thus Column A is 9. In Column B, you have to know how many nines there are in 72. To do that, divide 72 by 9: 72 ÷ 9 = 8; thus Column B is 8. Column A is greater than Column B, so the correct answer is A.

21 **Answer:** C

   Explanation: There are 12 months in a year, so Column A is equal to 12. A dozen is equal to 12, so there are 12 eggs in a dozen. The correct answer is C, since the two columns are equal.

22 **Answer:** A

   Explanation: The given in Column A is written in expanded form. To know the value, convert the expanded form to its standard form: 5000 + 400 + 60 + 7 + 0.2 + .05 = 5,467.25. Column A which is 5,467.25 is greater than 5,467.05, so the correct answer is A.

23 **Answer:** A

   Explanation: LCM is the short term for least common multiple. It is the smallest number that is a multiple of the given numbers. Prime factorization is one of the ways to find the LCM.

   $$\begin{array}{l} 6 - 2 \times 3 \\ 20 - 2 \times 2 \times 5 \\ \underline{36 - 2 \times 3 \times 2 \times 3} \\ 2 \times 3 \times 2 \times 3 \times 5 = 120 \end{array}$$

   The LCM of the numbers is 120, so Column A is 120. In Column B, to find the sum, just add the numbers: 6 + 20 + 36 = 62, so Column B is 62. The LCM which is 120 is greater than the sum which is 62; thus the correct answer is A.

24 **Answer:** B

   Explanation: Find the value in Column B. Add the numbers first, then find the square root of the sum: $\sqrt{(65+56)} = \sqrt{121} = 11$. Column B is 11 which is greater than 10, so the correct answer is B.

25 **Answer:** A

   Explanation: Remember that you can write out expression with exponent. In Column A, 2^7 can be written out as $2 \times 2 \times 2 \times 2 \times 2 \times 2 \times 2 = 128$. Column A is 128. The correct answer is A, since 128 is greater than 14.

26 **Answer:** A

   Explanation: Plug in the value for n. In Column A, find the remainder by dividing n by 7: 46 ÷ 7 = 6 r. 4, so Column A is 4. In Column B, divide n by 5: 46 ÷ 5 = 9 r. 1, so Column B is 1. Column A is greater than Column B; thus the correct answer is A.

27 **Answer:** C

   Explanation: For Column A, make an expression showing the number of students in class C. Based on the problem, the number of students in class C is 5 less than twice the number of students in class D considering that there are x students in class D. The words "less than" means to subtract and "twice" means to multiply by 2, so 5 less than twice the number of students in class D is equal to 2x − 5. The correct answer is C, since the two columns have the same expressions.

28 **Answer:** A

   Explanation: Find the value in each of the columns by finding the perimeter of the square. Remember that the formula in finding the perimeter of a square is P = 4s. In Column A, the length of the side is 4 m, substitute the value: P = 4(4 m) = 16 m. To compare, make them similar units by converting the perimeter of the square to cm: 16 × 100 cm = 1,600 cm. The correct answer is A, since Column A which is 1,600 cm is greater than 1,000 cm.

Grades 4–5 | Practice Test 2 Session 2

29 **Answer: B**

Explanation: Find the value in each of the column. In Column A, add the given numbers, since the phrase "more than" means to add: 1,225 + 2,345 = 3,570. Column A is 3,570. In Column B, multiply the numbers, since the word "times" means to multiply: 2,345 × 2 = 4,690. Column B is 4,690. The correct answer is B, since 4,690 is greater than 3,570.

30 **Answer: C**

Explanation: Find the total number of legs of the animals in each column. In Column A, the animal is a chicken and it has 2 legs. To find the total number of legs, multiply the number of chickens by the number of legs each chicken has: 12 × 2 = 24, so there are 24 legs in Column A. In Column B, the animal is a cow and it has 4 legs. To find the total number of legs, multiply the number of cows by the number of legs each cow has: 6 × 4 = 24, so there are 24 legs in Column B. The two columns are equal, so the correct answer is C.

31 **Answer: A**

Explanation: Write the number words in numerals. In Column A, one hundred thirty-six is written as 136. In Column B, one hundred thirty-seven thousandths is written as 0.137. The correct answer is A, since 136 is greater than 0.137.

32 **Answer: B**

Explanation: Plug in a value of an odd integer to evaluate the expression in each column. Let the odd integer be 9. In Column A, multiply the odd integer by 2 minus 6: (9 × 2) − 6 = 18 − 6 = 12. In Column B, multiply the odd integer by 3 minus 9: (9 × 3) − 9 = 27 − 9 = 18. The correct answer is B because whenever an odd integer is plugged into the expressions, Column B is greater than A.

33 **Answer: A**

Explanation: In Column A, there are three bags weighing 1.5 kilograms each. To find the total weight of the bags, multiply the number of bags by the weight of each bag: 3 × 1.5 kg = 4.5 kg. In Column B, there are two sacks weighing 2000 grams each. To find the total weight, multiply the number of sacks by the weight of each sack: 2 × 2000 g = 4,000 g. To compare, make them similar units. Convert the total weight of bags to grams: 4.5 × 1,000 = 4,500 grams. Column A is 4,500 grams which is greater than 4,000 grams, so the correct answer is A.

34 **Answer: B**

Explanation: Plug in a value of an odd integer. Odd integers are numbers that cannot be divided exactly into half. For instance, let the odd integer be 7. In Column A, multiply the odd integer by 6, then minus 7: (7 × 6) − 7 = 42 − 7 = 35. In Column B, multiply the odd integer by 7, then minus 6: (7 × 7) − 6 = 49 − 7 = 42. The correct answer is B because 42 is greater than 35.

35 **Answer: C**

Explanation: Prime are numbers whose only factor is 1 and the number itself. In Column A, the prime factors of 36 are 2 and 3, so its greatest prime factor is 3. In Column B, the prime factors of 48 are 2 and 3, so its greatest prime factor is 3 also. The correct answer is C, since the two columns are equal.

36 **Answer: A**

Explanation: Column A contains Vexana's present age. To find her age, add 5 to Odette's age, since she is 5 years older than her: 12 + 5 = 17. Column B contains Odette's age in 3 years. To find her age, add 3 to her present's age: 12 + 3 = 15. The correct answer is A, since 17 is greater than 15.

37 **Answer: B**

Explanation: In Column B, $(201.70)^2$ can also be written out as 201.70 × 201.70 = 40,682.89. Column B which is equal to 40,682.89 is greater than 4,000, so the correct answer is B.

38 **Answer:** A

Explanation: Probability refers to the chance of an event to happen. The formula in finding the probability is $\frac{\text{number of events to happen}}{\text{number of possible outcomes}}$. In Column A, the number of events to happen is 10, since there are 10 green marbles and the number of possible outcomes is 29, since there are 29 marbles in total (12 + 7 + 10 = 29). Column A is $\frac{10}{29}$. In Column B, the number of events to happen is 7, since there are 7 blue marbles and the number of possible outcomes is 29. Column B is $\frac{7}{29}$. Column A is greater than Column B; thus the correct answer is A.

39 **Answer:** B

Explanation: Plug in values to the letters. Notice that the value of A is less than C and B and the value of C and B is greater than D such as D is greater than 0. For instance, let A be 4, C be 6, B be 7 and D be 2. Plug in the values in each expression in the column. In Column A, A – B = 4 – 7 = –3. In Column B, C – D = 6 – 2 = 4. The correct answer is B because whenever such values are plugged into the expressions, Column B is always greater than A.

40 **Answer:** A

Explanation: Find the number of revolutions that the windmill made in 3 minutes given that each revolution takes 15 seconds. There are two steps to find the answer. First, find out how many seconds there are in 3 minutes. To do that, multiply the number of minutes by 60, since there are 60 seconds in a minute: 3 × 60 = 180 seconds. Second, divide it by 15 seconds: 60 ÷ 15 = 4. There are 4 revolutions in 3 minutes. The correct answer is A, since 6 is greater than 4.

41 **Answer:** C

Explanation: Find the value in each of the column by finding the percentage of the numbers. The word "of" means to multiply and make the percent as a decimal number. In Column A, find the 15 percent of 90: 0.15 × 90 = 13.5. In Column B, find the 90 percent of 15: 0.90 × 15 = 13.5. The two columns are equal, so the correct answer is C.

42 **Answer:** C

Explanation: Add the fractions in Column A. Since the fractions are similar, just add the numerators and copy the denominator. Simplify the answer, if possible: $\frac{4}{5} + \frac{4}{5} = \frac{8}{5}$ or $1\frac{3}{5}$. Column A and Column B are equal to $1\frac{3}{5}$, so the correct answer is C.

43 **Answer:** A

Explanation: Median refers to the middle number in a list. To find the median in Column A, arrange the numbers in increasing order first: 12, 6, 7, 15, 11 = 6, 7, 11, 15, 12. Since there are five numbers in the list, the median is the one in the middle which is 11. Column A is 11. Then in Column B, mean refers to the average of the numbers. To find mean, add the numbers and divide the sum by 5: 12 + 6 + 7 + 15 + 11 = 51 ÷ 5 = 10.2. Column B is 10.2. 11 is greater than 10.2; so the correct answer is A.

44 **Answer:** B

Explanation: The sum of the interior angles of a triangle is 180°. To find the value of x in Column A, add the two given angles and subtract it from 180°: 180° - (115° + 37°) = 180° – 152° = 28°. Column A is 28°. The correct answer is B, since 45° is greater than 28°.

45 **Answer:** C

Explanation: Round off the given numbers to find the value in each of the column. Remember the rules in rounding numbers: if the digit next to the rounding digit is 4, 3, 2, 1, or 0, round down; if the digit next to the rounding digit is 5, 6, 7, 8, or 9, round up. In Column A, the rounding digit in 75,356 is the hundreds place which is 3. The digit next to it is 5, so round up: 75,400. In Column B, the rounding digit in 75,404 is the tens place which is 0. The digit next to it is 4, so round down: 75,400. The two columns are equal, so the correct answer is C.

| Grades 4–5 | Practice Test 2 Session 2 |

46 **Answer: C**

Explanation: Column A contains the greatest fraction which is $\frac{6}{7}$. Column B contains the product of the smallest fraction and $\frac{3}{7}$: $\frac{2}{7} \times \frac{3}{7} = \frac{6}{7}$. The two columns are both $\frac{6}{7}$, so the correct answer is C.

47 **Answer: B**

Explanation: Find the number of hours in Column A by subtracting the starting hour from the ending hour: 10:45 – 6:30 = 4:15. Column A is 4 hours and 15 minutes. The correct answer is B, since 4 hours and 25 minutes is greater than 4 hours and 15 minutes.

48 **Answer: A**

Explanation: Column A contains the square root of 30. Since the lower perfect square number that is nearest to 30 is 25, find its square root: $\sqrt{25} = 5$. Since its square root is 5, the square root of 30 lies between the integers 5 and 6. Column B contains the greatest prime factor of 30 which is 5. The square root of 30 is greater than 5, so the correct answer is A.

49 **Answer: C**

Explanation: Column A reads 0.75 hour. To find how much of an hour it is, multiply it by 60, since there are 60 minutes in an hour: 0.75 × 60 = 45 minutes. The two columns are both 45 minutes, so the correct answer is C.

50 **Answer: B**

Explanation: In Column A, the digit 5 is in the thousandths place, so its value is 0.005. In Column B, 5 hundredths can also be written as 0.05. The correct answer is B, since 0.05 is greater than 0.005.

51 **Answer: C**

Explanation: Apply the PEMDAS rule to evaluate each expression. In Column A, work with the parentheses first: (12 + 20) × 15 ÷ 3 = 32 × 15 ÷ 3. There is no exponent, so do multiplication and division from left to right: 32 × 15 ÷ 3 = 480 ÷ 3 = 160. Column A is 160. In Column B, work with the parentheses first: (12 + 20) × (15 ÷ 3) = 32 × 5. There is no exponent, so do multiplication and division from left to right: 32 × 5 = 160. Column B is 160 also. Since the two columns are equal, the correct answer is C.

52 **Answer: B**

Explanation: Find the number of children there are in the movie theater by subtracting the sum of the number of women and men from the total number of people in the theater: 150 – (75 + 60) = 150 – 135 = 15. Column A is 15. The correct answer is B, since 50 is greater than 15.

53 **Answer: B**

Explanation: When multiplying decimals by a power of 10, just move the decimal point to the right. In Column A, multiplying by 10^5 means you have to move the decimal point in 16.5 five places to the right to get 1,650,000. In Column B, multiplying by 10^7 means you have to move the decimal point in 0.165 seven places to the right to get 1,650,000. Both columns are 1,650,000, so the correct answer is C.

54 **Answer: B**

Explanation: Column A contains the number of dogs in the pet store. Find the number of dogs using the equation 5x + 3x = 96. Combine similar terms first: 8x = 96. Divide both sides by 8: $\frac{8x}{8} = \frac{96}{8}$ = x = 12. Substitute the value of x in 5x, since 5x of the animals are dogs: 5(12) = 60. The correct answer is B, since 65 is greater than 60.

55 **Answer: A**

Explanation: In Column A, distribute 5 in the expression 5(4x + 6) to get 20x + 30. In Column B, distribute 4 in the expression 4(5x + 6) to get 20x + 24. Since there is a variable, plug in a value for x. Let x be 3. For Column A, 20x + 30 = 20(3) + 30 = 60 + 30 = 90. For Column B, 20x + 24 = 20(3) + 24 = 60 + 24 = 84. The correct answer is A, because whenever a value is plugged into the variable, Column A is greater than Column B.

Practice Test 3

Verbal Practice Test

> **Directions:**
>
> Each question begins with two words. These two words go together in a certain way. Under them, there are four other pairs of words lettered A, B, C, and D.
>
> Find the lettered pair of words that go together in the same way as the first pair of words.

1 odometer: speed

   A. seismograph: earthquake

   B. scale: heavy

   C. thermometer: degree

   D. protractor: length

Answer:

2 deer: fawn

   A. dog: snoopy

   B. swan: cygnet

   C. cock: hen

   D. man: woman

Answer:

3 cricket: pitch

   A. basketball: field

   B. soccer: net

   C. wrestling: arena

   D. bowling: court

Answer:

4 junk: trash

    A. life: journey

    B. bin: garbage

    C. junket: trip

    D. chest: diamond

Answer:

5 smear: libel

    A. heed: consider

    B. arid: fertile

    C. peerless: equal

    D. failure: mistake

Answer:

6 principal: student

    A. king: queen

    B. vendor: buyer

    C. marshal: prisoner

    D. architect: carpenter

Answer:

7 partition: divide

    A. conjugate: pair

    B. parade: festival

    C. wedding: couple

    D. group: share

Answer:

8 principle: doctrine

    A. famous: obscure

    B. living: livelihood

    C. passage: message

    D. rule: verdict

Answer:

9 alphabetical: list

   A. order: sort

   B. exercise: jog

   C. sequential: files

   D. arrangement: part

Answer:

10 geology: rocks

   A. psychology: physician

   B. biology: body

   C. chronology: chronicle

   D. cytology: cells

Answer:

11 flash: camera

   A. mouse: computer

   B. light: picture

   C. flower: insect

   D. nest: bird

Answer:

12 cool: freeze

   A. heat: oven

   B. moisten: soak

   C. vitamin: grow

   D. cold: water

Answer:

13 herd: cow

   A. ocean: porpoise

   B. flock: fish

   C. pod: dolphin

   D. neigh: horse

Answer:

Grades 4–5   Practice Test 3 Session 1

14 lion: lioness

    A. master: mister

    B. prince: princes

    C. wizard: witch

    D. ten: tennis

Answer:

15 frog: tadpole

    A. kitten: kitty

    B. horse: foal

    C. tiger: tigress

    D. monkey: gorilla

Answer:

16 shirt: garment

    A. rat: rodent

    B. shorts: pants

    C. socks: mittens

    D. headband: hair

Answer:

17 microscope: magnify

    A. razor: hair

    B. shovel: shave

    C. spade: dig

    D. spoon: fork

Answer:

18 whisper: shout

    A. resonant: audible

    B. sloth: action

    C. slim: bulky

    D. expand: create

Answer:

Grades 4–5 Practice Test 3 Session 1

19 create: destroy
    A. itchy: scratch
    B. advance: retreat
    C. drizzle: typhoon
    D. tropical: cold

Answer:

20 fallacy: illusion
    A. brim: edge
    B. lonely: depressed
    C. magnificent: superior
    D. accomplished: lectured

Answer:

21 pupils: class
    A. teacher: school
    B. people: countries
    C. rioters: gang
    D. singer: chorus

Answer:

22 circle: arc
    A. pen: nib
    B. window: door
    C. curtain: cloth
    D. curve: triangle

Answer:

23 omelette: egg
    A. bottle: paper
    B. road: asphalt
    C. sandwich: lettuce
    D. cucumber: catsup

Answer:

24 scientist: experiment

    A. basketball: pool

    B. doctor: medicine

    C. actor: play

    D. singer: choreograph

Answer:

25 detective: clues

    A. hunter: insects

    B. swimmer: water

    C. player: music

    D. pig: truffles

Answer:

26 sloth: action

    A. unscrupulousness: principles

    B. love: affection

    C. sadness: depression

    D. kiss: smack

Answer:

27 brief: court case

    A. judge: law

    B. hypothesis: guess

    C. experiment: laboratory

    D. abstract: research paper

Answer:

28 serve: tennis

    A. dribble: volleyball

    B. drive: golf

    C. travelling: soccer

    D. shoot: dart

Answer:

29 dove: peace

   A. mouse: coward

   B. lion: courage

   C. dog: friend

   D. elephant: arrogant

Answer:

30 grove: forest

   A. pond: lake

   B. river: ocean

   C. mountain: plateau

   D. plains: canyon

Answer:

31 tumbler: mug

   A. pan: cake

   B. towel: pot holder

   C. trowel: spade

   D. curtain: refrigerator

Answer:

32 crumb: bread

   A. atom: molecule

   B. roof: bedroom

   C. sugar: condiment

   D. phone: message

Answer:

33 collar: shirt

   A. purse: wallet

   B. visor: hat

   C. umbrella: raincoat

   D. bottle: plastic

Answer:

34 apology: forgiveness

    A. reward: punishment

    B. present: celebration

    C. bribe: influence

    D. sorry: thankful

Answer:

35 cluster: stars

    A. planet: mars

    B. satellite: moons

    C. bunch: birds

    D. thicket: shrubs

Answer:

36 rake: grass

    A. census: information

    B. fork: soup

    C. dip: sauce

    D. story: experience

Answer:

37 telescope: stars

    A. periscope: ships

    B. magnify: glass

    C. flashlight: light

    D. microscope: observe

Answer:

38 tarpaulin: rain

    A. towel: water

    B. apron: stains

    C. napkin: dirt

    D. frame: picture

Answer:

Grades 4–5 Practice Test 3 Session 1

39 cellar: house

  A. attic: home
  B. scarecrow: garden
  C. hold: ship
  D. sail: sailboat

Answer:

40 throne: king

  A. bench: judge
  B. swing: kid
  C. palace: knight
  D. chair: baby

Answer:

41 hook: coat

  A. needle: thread
  B. thumbtack: poster
  C. pin: cloth
  D. nail: stick

Answer:

42 murmur: sound

  A. grain: field
  B. broom: sweep
  C. chew: digestion
  D. stratus: cloud

Answer:

43 buoy: channel

  A. flare: accident
  B. floater: pool
  C. soap: body
  D. flame: wildfire

Answer:

44 fist: hand

    A. store: stuff

    B. circuit: loop

    C. skull: head

    D. ankle: foot

Answer:

45 unseen: invisible

    A. elegant: cheap

    B. blurred: visible

    C. shocked: excited

    D. risible: funny

Answer:

46 mythical: historical

    A. general: particular

    B. friendly: funny

    C. magical: powerful

    D. essential: necessary

Answer:

47 carat: diamond

    A. pound: heavy

    B. caliber: bullet

    C. paint: mural

    D. exhibit: artifact

Answer:

48 viaduct: water

    A. artery: blood

    B. mountain: land

    C. pigeon: air

    D. pineapple: juice

Answer:

Grades 4–5 Practice Test 3 Session 1

49 crust: bread

   A. snack: sandwich

   B. Hawaiian: pizza

   C. wattle: neck

   D. water: mouth

Answer:

50 painter: gallery

   A. sculptor: stone

   B. driver: transportation

   C. pilot: travel

   D. gambler: casino

Answer:

51 sparrow: chirp

   A. duck: duckling

   B. tiger: cub

   C. lion: shout

   D. camel: grunt

Answer:

52 imaginary: real

   A. hostile: friendly

   B. suggest: advice

   C. truth: reality

   D. practice: perfect

Answer:

53 chapter: book

   A. sentence: message

   B. charge: battery

   C. precinct: city

   D. peak: mountain

Answer:

54 shard: glass

  A. smoke: fire

  B. cinder: ash

  C. latex: paint

  D. cotton: fabric

Answer:

55 astronomer: space

  A. astronaut: spaceship

  B. swimmer: tide

  C. spelunker: caves

  D. seller: product

Answer:

Optional Break

Quantitative Practice Test

Directions:

Each question given below has two parts. One part is column A, the other part is column B. You must find out if one part is greater than the other, or if the parts are equal, you will choose one answer.

A. If the part in column A is greater

B. If the part in column B is greater

C. The two parts are equal

Question 1

Column A	Column B
5^6	10,000

Answer:

Question 2

In a class of 50 students, 60 percent of the students study French.

Column A	Column B
The number of students who study French	30

Answer:

Question 3

Column A	Column B
Four more than the product of twelve and 7	80

Answer:

Question 4

Column A	Column B
The area of a square whose side is 25 cm long	The perimeter of a 16 cm by 12 cm rectangle

Answer:

Question 5

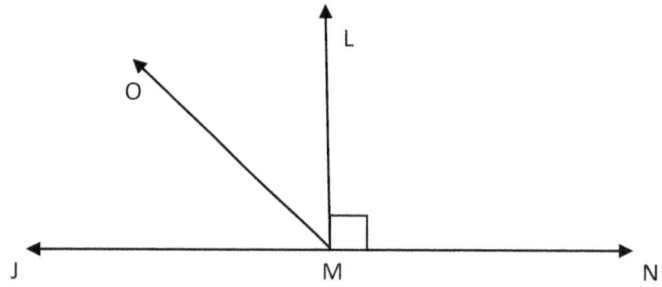

Column A	Column B
The measure of angle LMN	The measure of angle OMJ

Answer:

Question 6

Column A	Column B
The number of sixes in 66	The number of twos in 22

Answer:

Question 7

Mr. Cruz sells fruit in the market. Banana costs $1.5 per kilogram and grape costs $2.5 per kilogram.

Column A	Column B
The total cost of 6 kilograms of bananas	The total cost of 3 kilograms of grapes

Answer:

Grades 4–5   Practice Test 3 Session 2

Question 8

Column A	Column B
The value of 6 in 12.678	The value of 1 in 321.9

Answer:

Question 9

Column A	Column B
22(3w − 4n)	66w − 88n

Answer:

Question 10

Column A	Column B
The sum of the three consecutive even integers from 22	The sum of the three consecutive odd integers from 21

Answer:

Question 11

Column A	Column B
The number of years from 1898 to 2020	128

Answer:

Question 12

Column A	Column B
The distance between the tips of the hour and minute hands of a clock at nine o'clock	The distance between the tips of the hour and minute hands of the same clock at nine fifteen

Answer:

Question 13

Column A	Column B
$3 \times 10^3 + 2 \times 10^2 + 10$	321×10

Answer:

Question 14

Column A	Column B
The number of sides of a hexagon	The number of sides of an octagon

Answer:

Question 15

$z < 0$

Column A	Column B
$46z$	$4z \times 6z$

Answer:

Question 16

Column A	Column B
$\sqrt{0.36}$	$\sqrt{0.0036}$

Answer:

Question 17

Column A	Column B
$6 \times (4 + 12) - 12$	$(6 \times 4 + 12) - 12$

Answer:

Question 18

h > k

Column A	Column B
30% of h	50% of k

Answer: _____

Question 19

Column A	Column B
The GCF of 14, 35 and 21	8

Answer: _____

Question 20

Column A	Column B
$\frac{4}{7} \times \frac{3}{4}$	$\frac{4}{8} \times \frac{1}{2}$

Answer: _____

Question 21

Column A	Column B
Largest factor of 100	Smallest positive multiple of 100

Answer: _____

Question 22

Column A	Column B
75 × 3	35 + 35 + 35 + 35 + 35

Answer: _____

Question 23

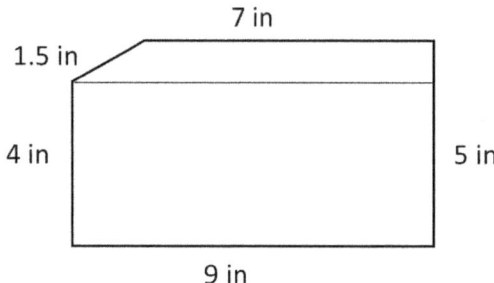

Column A	Column B
The perimeter of the pentagon	The perimeter of the rectangle

Answer:

Question 24

Eeva had 68 points correct out of a total of 85 points in her Math test.

Column A	Column B
Eeva's percentage grade	68%

Answer:

Question 25

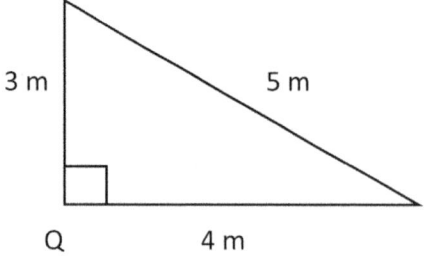

Column A	Column B
The area of ΔQ	9 sq m

Answer:

Question 26

x > 5

Column A	Column B
Five less than x	5 - x

Answer:

Question 27

x + 4 = −14

Column A	Column B
−10	x

Answer:

Question 28

The ratio of rabbits to squirrels is 2:3. There are a total of 225 rabbits and squirrels.

Column A	Column B
The number of squirrels	120

Answer:

Question 29

Column A	Column B
The total number of feet of 23 ducks	The total number of wheels of 15 cars

Answer:

Grades 4–5 | Practice Test 3 Session 2

Question 30

Set A: {50, 78, 88, 92}

Set B: {67, 89, 92, 94}

Column A	Column B
The mean of set A	The median of set B

Answer:

Question 31

The sale price for a snowboard is $63. This price reflects a 30% discount.

Column A	Column B
The original price of the snowboard	$90

Answer:

Question 32

Column A	Column B
The number of years in a century	The number of years in a decade

Answer:

Question 33

$y > 0$

Column A	Column B
$\dfrac{5}{y}$	$\dfrac{y}{9}$

Answer:

Question 34

There are 146 athletes and 8 coaches taking a trip to a competition. They travel in buses that seat 48 people.

Column A	Column B
The number of buses needed	4

Answer:

Question 35

Column A	Column B
$\dfrac{6}{12} \div \dfrac{2}{7}$	1.75

Answer:

Question 36

Column A	Column B
One hundred twenty-five thousandths	125,000

Answer:

Question 37

24, 45, 16, 32, 5, 73, 65, 91, 12, 34

Column A	Column B
The sum of the even integers	The sum of the odd integers

Answer:

Question 38

Jonathan has 345 marbles. Two-fifths of them are white marbles.

Column A	Column B
The number of white marbles	150

Answer:

Question 39

z = 12

Column A	Column B
(34)(5z)	(34z)(5)

Answer:

Question 40

Column A	Column B
p^2	$-p^2$

Answer:

Question 41

Column A	Column B
Hours in a day	Seconds in a minute

Answer:

Question 42

r > 0

Column A	Column B
$5\sqrt{3r}$	$3\sqrt{5r}$

Answer:

Question 43

Column A	Column B
The quotient of 558 and 9	61

Answer:

Question 44

Column A	Column B
The number of primes between 40 and 50	The number of primes between 1 and 6

Answer:

Question 45

Gab is driving at a steady rate of 56 miles per hour

Column A	Column B
Number of minutes it will take Gab to drive 42 miles	45 minutes

Answer:

Question 46

Column A	Column B
The difference between 123,456 and 678	The difference between 123,456 and 786

Answer:

Question 47

Column A	Column B
Square of 9	Square root of 121

Answer:

Question 48

Notebook - $1.5

Box of Crayons - $2

Bag - $12

Pad Paper - $1

Column A	Column B
The total cost of two notebooks and a bag	The total cost of a bag, pad paper and a box of crayons

Answer:

Question 49

Column A	Column B
$1^{17} + 2^3$	25

Answer:

Question 50

$5x + 3 = 18$

Column A	Column B
x	3

Answer:

Question 51

Radius = 23 cm

1 m = 100 cm

Column A	Column B
The circumference of the circle	2 m

Answer:

Question 52

Column A	Column B
$\frac{3}{4}(12+48)-25$	30

Answer:

Question 53

Column A	Column B
Three hundredths	$\frac{3}{100}$

Answer:

Question 54

Column A	Column B
30,000 + 400 + 20 + 5 + 0.004	30,000 + 400 + 20 + 0.5 + 0.004

Answer:

Question 55

Column A	Column B
The slope of the line $y = 2x - 3$	The slope of the line $y = \frac{1}{2}x + 3$

Answer:

Answer Key

Verbal

1	A	29	B
2	B	30	A
3	C	31	C
4	C	32	A
5	A	33	B
6	C	34	C
7	A	35	D
8	B	36	A
9	C	37	C
10	C	38	B
11	A	39	C
12	B	40	A
13	C	41	B
14	C	42	D
15	B	43	A
16	A	44	B
17	C	45	D
18	C	46	A
19	B	47	B
20	A	48	A
21	D	49	C
22	A	50	D
23	B	51	D
24	B	52	A
25	D	53	C
26	A	54	B
27	D	55	C
28	B		

Quantitative

1	A	29	B
2	C	30	B
3	A	31	C
4	A	32	A
5	A	33	B
6	C	34	C
7	A	35	C
8	B	36	B
9	C	37	B
10	A	38	B
11	B	39	C
12	B	40	C
13	C	41	B
14	B	42	A
15	B	43	A
16	A	44	C
17	A	45	C
18	A	46	A
19	B	47	A
20	C	48	C
21	C	49	B
22	A	50	C
23	A	51	B
24	A	52	B
25	B	53	C
26	A	54	A
27	A	55	A
28	A		

Answer Key with Explanations

Verbal

1 **Answer:** A

Explanation: An odometer is used to measure speed and a seismograph is used to measure earthquake.

2 **Answer:** B

Explanation: A fawn is the young one of a deer and a cygnet is the young one of a swan.

3 **Answer:** C

Explanation: A cricket is played in the pitch, while a wrestling is played in the arena.

4 **Answer:** C

Explanation: A junk is a synonym of trash and a junket is a synonym of trip.

5 **Answer:** A

Explanation: To smear is a synonym of libel and to heed is a synonym of to consider.

6 **Answer:** C

Explanation: A principal is the person in charge of a student, while a marshal is the person in charge of a prisoner.

7 **Answer:** A

Explanation: To partition means to divide and to conjugate means to pair.

8 **Answer:** B

Explanation: A principle is another word for a doctrine and a living is another word for a livelihood.

9 **Answer:** C

Explanation: Alphabetical describes the ordering of list, while sequential describes the ordering of files.

10 **Answer:** C

Explanation: Geology is the study of rocks and a cytology is the study of cells.

11 **Answer:** A

Explanation: A flash is part of a camera and a mouse is part of a computer.

12 **Answer:** B

Explanation: To cool is to lessen the temperature less intensely than to freeze and to moisten is to wet less intensely than to soak.

13 **Answer:** C

Explanation: A group of cows is called a herd and a group of dolphins is called a pod.

14 **Answer:** C

Explanation: A lion is the male, while a lioness is the female. A wizard is the male, while a witch is the female.

Grades 4–5   Practice Test 3 Session 1

15. **Answer: B**
   Explanation: A tadpole is a baby frog and a foal is a baby horse.

16. **Answer: A**
   Explanation: A shirt belongs to the class of garment and rat belongs to the class of rodent.

17. **Answer: C**
   Explanation: A microscope is used to magnify and a spade is used to dig.

18. **Answer: C**
   Explanation: The opposite of whisper is shout and the opposite of slim is bulky.

19. **Answer: B**
   Explanation: The opposite of create is to destroy and the opposite of advance is retreat.

20. **Answer: A**
   Explanation: The synonym of fallacy is illusion and the synonym of brim is edge.

21. **Answer: D**
   Explanation: The group of pupils is called class and the group of singers is called chorus.

22. **Answer: A**
   Explanation: A part of circle is arc and a part of pen is nib.

23. **Answer: B**
   Explanation: An omelette is made of egg and the road is made of asphalt.

24. **Answer: B**
   Explanation: A scientist performs an experiment, and an actor performs a play.

25. **Answer: D**
   Explanation: A detective hunts for clues, and a pig hunts for truffles.

26. **Answer: A**
   Explanation: Sloth is a lack of action, and unscrupulousness is a lack of principles.

27. **Answer: D**
   Explanation: A brief is a summary of short case, and an abstract is a summary of a research paper.

28. **Answer: B**
   Explanation: A serve is an action in tennis, and drive is an action in golf.

29. **Answer: B**
   Explanation: A dove is a symbol of peace, and a lion is a symbol of courage.

30. **Answer: A**
   Explanation: A grove is a smaller version of forest, and a pond is a smaller version of lake.

31. **Answer: C**
   Explanation: Both tumbler and mug are used for drinking and trowel and spades are used for gardening.

32	Answer: A
	Explanation: A crumb is a part of bread and an atom is a part of molecule.
33	Answer: B
	Explanation: A collar is a part of shirt and a visor is a part of hat.
34	Answer: C
	Explanation: An apology is used to attain forgiveness and a bribe is used to attain influence.
35	Answer: D
	Explanation: A cluster is a group of stars, while a thicket is a group of shrubs.
36	Answer: A
	Explanation: A rake is used to gather grass and a census is used to gather information.
37	Answer: C
	Explanation: A telescope is used to look for stars and a periscope is used to look for ships.
38	Answer: B
	Explanation: A tarpaulin is used to protect from rain, while an apron is used to protect from stains.
39	Answer: C
	Explanation: A cellar is a lower storage area in a house and a hold is a lower storage area in a ship.
40	Answer: A
	Explanation: A throne is the seat of a king, while a judge sits on a bench.
41	Answer: B
	Explanation: A hook is used to hang a coat as a thumbtack is used to hang a poster.
42	Answer: D
	Explanation: A murmur is a low sound, while a stratus is a type of low cloud.
43	Answer: A
	Explanation: A buoy is used to mark a channel, while a flare is used to mark an accident.
44	Answer: B
	Explanation: A fist is a closed hand and a circuit is a closed loop.
45	Answer: D
	Explanation: Unseen is a synonym of invisible and risible is a synonym of funny
46	Answer: A
	Explanation: Something that is mythical is not historical and something that is not general is particular.
47	Answer: B
	Explanation: A carat is a measurement of a diamond, while a caliber is a measurement of a bullet.
48	Answer: A
	Explanation: A viaduct carries water and an artery carries blood.

49	**Answer:** C
	Explanation: A crust is part of a bread and a wattle is part of a neck.
50	**Answer:** D
	Explanation: A painter works in a gallery, while a gambler works in a casino.
51	**Answer:** D
	Explanation: A chirp is a sound produced by sparrow, while a grunt is a sound produced by camel.
52	**Answer:** A
	Explanation: Imaginary is the opposite of real and hostile is the opposite of friendly.
53	**Answer:** C
	Explanation: A chapter is a division of a book and a precinct is a division of a city.
54	**Answer:** B
	Explanation: A shard is a fragment of glass and a cinder is a fragment of ash.
55	**Answer:** C
	Explanation: An astronomer is someone who explores space, while a spelunker is someone who explores caves.

Quantitative

1. **Answer:** A

   Explanation: Remember that you can write out expression with exponent. In Column A, 5^6 can be written out as $5 \times 5 \times 5 \times 5 \times 5 \times 5 = 15{,}625$. Column A which is 15,625 is greater than 10,000, so the correct answer is A.

2. **Answer:** C

   Explanation: Column A contains the number of students who study French. To find the number of students, get the 60% of 50. Remember that the word "of" means to multiply and the percent should be changed to decimal: $50 \times 0.60 = 30$. The two columns are equal, so the correct answer is C.

3. **Answer:** A

   Explanation: Translate the mathematical sentence into an equation, then solve. In Column A, four more than the product of twelve and 7 is $(12 \times 7) + 4 = 84 + 4 = 88$. Column A which is 88 is greater than Column B which is 80, so the correct answer is A.

4. **Answer:** A

   Explanation: The formula in finding the area of a square is $A = s^2$. In Column A, the side of the square is 25 cm: $A = (25 \text{ cm})^2 = 625$ cm. The formula in finding the perimeter of a rectangle is $P = 2L + 2W$. In Column B, the dimensions of the rectangle is 16 cm by 12 cm: $P = 2(16 \text{ cm}) + 2(12 \text{ cm}) = 32 \text{ cm} + 24 \text{ Cm} = 56$ cm. ^25 is greater than 56, so the correct answer is A.

5. **Answer:** A

   Explanation: Column A contains the angle LMN which is a right angle, so it measures 90°. Column B contains the angle OMJ which is an acute angle, so it measures less than 90°. A right angle is greater than an acute angle, so the correct answer is A.

6   **Answer: C**

   Explanation: Column A contains the number of sixes in 66, divide 66 by 6 to get 11. Column B contains the number of twos in 22, divide to get 11. The two columns are equal, so the correct answer is C.

7   **Answer: A**

   Explanation: Find the total cost in each column. In Column A, multiply the cost of banana per kilogram by the number of kilos: $1.5 × 6 = $9. In Column B, multiply the cost of grape per kilogram by the number of kilos: $2.5 × 3 = $7.5. $9 is greater than $7.5, so the correct answer is A.

8   **Answer: B**

   Explanation: In Column A, the place value of digit 6 in 12.678 is tenths, so its value is 0.6. In Column B, the place value of 1 in 321.9 is ones, so its value is 1. 1 is greater than 0.6, so the correct answer is B.

9   **Answer: C**

   Explanation: In Column A, distribute 22 in the expression 22(3w − 4n) to get 66w − 88n. The expressions in two columns are the same, thus the correct answer is C.

10   **Answer: A**

   Explanation: Even integers are numbers that can be divided exactly into half, while odd integers are numbers that cannot be divided exactly into half. Column A contains the sum of the three consecutive even integers from 22: 22 + 24 + 26 = 72. Column B contains the sum of the three consecutive odd integers from 21: 21 + 23 + 25 = 69. Column A is greater than Column B, therefore the correct answer is A.

11   **Answer: B**

   Explanation: In Column A, to find the number of years from 1898 to 2020, subtract: 2020 − 1898 = 122. Column B which is 128 is greater than 122, so the correct answer is B.

12   **Answer: B**

   Explanation: To compare, identify the angles formed by the hands of the clock during the given time. In Column A, the minute hand is at 12 and the hour hand is at 9 which formed a right angle, so Column A is equal to 90°. In Column B, the minute hand is at 3 and the hour hand is at 9 which formed a straight angle, so Column B is equal to 180°. The correct answer is B, since a straight angle is greater than a right angle.

13   **Answer: C**

   Explanation: Write the number in Column A in standard form. Remember that when multiplying by a power of 10, the exponent denotes the number of zeros to add. In Column A, $3 \times 10^3 + 2 \times 10^2 + 10 = 3000 + 200 + 10 = 3,210$. In Column B, just multiply: 321 × 10 = 3,210. The two columns are equal, so the correct answer is C.

14   **Answer: B**

   Explanation: Column A is equal to 6, since hexagon is a polygon with 6 sides. Column B is equal to 8, since octagon is a polygon with 8 sides. 8 is greater than 6, so the correct answer is B.

15   **Answer: B**

   Explanation: Plug in a value for z. Notice that the value of z should be less than 0 or a negative number. For instance, z is −3. Substitute the value of z in each expression. In Column A, 46z = 46(−3) = −138. In Column B, 4z × 6z = 4(−3) × 6(−3) = −12 × −18 = 216. Column B is greater than Column A. The correct answer is B because whenever a negative value is plugged into the expressions, Column B is always greater than Column A.

16   **Answer: A**

   Explanation: In Column A, the square root of 0.36 is 0.6. In Column B, the square root of 0.0036 is 0.06. The correct answer is A, since 0.6 is greater than 0.06.

17 Answer: A

Explanation: Apply the PEMDAS rule. In Column A, work with the parentheses first: 6 × (4 + 12) – 12 = 6 × 16 – 12. There is no exponent, so do the multiplication and division from left to right: 6 × 16 – 12 = 96 – 12. Lastly, do the addition and subtraction from left to right: 96 – 12 = 84. Column A is 84. In Column B, work with the parentheses first: (6 × 4 + 12) – 12 = 36 – 12. There are no exponents and multiplication and division, so do the addition and subtraction from left to right: 36 – 12 = 24. Column B is 24. Column A is greater than Column B; thus the correct answer is A.

18 Answer: A

Explanation: There are variables involved, so plug in a value for h and k. Notice that the value of h is greater than k. For instance, let h be 80 and k be 40. In Column A, plug in 80 in the expression: 30% of 80 = 0.30 × 80 = 24. In Column B, plug in 40 in the expression: 50% of 40 = 0.50 × 40 = 20. 24 is greater than 20; therefore the correct answer is A.

19 Answer: B

Explanation: GCF is the highest factor that the numbers have in common. List down the factors of each number: 14 = 1, 2, 7, 14; 35 = 1, 5, 7, 35; 21 = 1, 3, 7, 21. Column A is 7. 8 is greater than 7, so the correct answer is B.

20 Answer: C

Explanation: To multiply fractions, multiply the numerators across and the denominators across. Simplify, if possible. In Column A, $\frac{4}{7} \times \frac{3}{4} = \frac{12}{48}$ or $\frac{1}{4}$. In Column B, $\frac{4}{8} \times \frac{1}{2} = \frac{4}{16}$ or $\frac{1}{4}$. The two columns are equal, so the correct answer is C.

21 Answer: C

Explanation: Factors refer to the numbers that when multiplied is equal to another number. In Column A, the largest factor of 100 is 100, since 1 × 100 = 100. Then, multiples refer to the result of multiplying two numbers together. In Column B, the smallest positive multiple of 100 is 100, since 100 × 1 = 100. The two columns are equal; thus the correct answer is C.

22 Answer: A

Explanation: Evaluate each expression. In Column A, 75 × 3 = 225. In Column B, 35 + 35 + 35 + 35 + 35 = 175. 225 is greater than 175; therefore the correct answer is A.

23 Answer: A

Explanation: Perimeter refers to the distance around a figure. For Column A, to find the perimeter of the pentagon, add all the measure of its sides: 7 in + 1.5 in + 4 in + 5 in + 9 in = 26.5 in. For Column B, to find the perimeter of the rectangle, use the formula P = 2L + 2W: 2(9 in) + 2(4 in) = 18 in + 8 in = 26 in. The correct answer is A, since 26.5 is greater than 26.

24 Answer: A

Explanation: Eeva's percentage grade is the ratio of the number of correct answers to the total number of points on the test, multiplied by 100. This is $\frac{68}{85} \times 100 = 0.8 \times 100 = 80\%$. Column A which is 80% is greater than Column B which is 68%, so the correct answer is A.

25 Answer: B

Explanation: The formula used to find the area of a triangle is $A = \frac{1}{2} bh$, where b is the base and h is the height. For Column A, the base of ΔQ is 4 m and the height is 3 m. Plug in the triangle's dimensions: $\frac{1}{2} (4 \text{ m})(3 \text{ m}) = \frac{1}{2} (12 \text{ sq m}) = 6$ sq m. The correct answer is B, since 9 sq m is greater than 6 sq m.

26 **Answer: A**

   Explanation: Plug in a value for x. Notice that x is greater than 5. For instance, x be 7. In Column A, five less than x can be written as x – 5. Plug in the value: 7 – 5 = 2. Column A is 2. In Column B, 5 – x: 5 – 7 = –2. Column B is –2. The correct answer is A, because whenever a value greater than 5 is plugged into the expressions, Column A is equal to a positive number which is greater than Column B, a negative number.

27 **Answer: A**

   Explanation: To evaluate the given expression, subtract 4 from both sides: x + 4 – 4 = –14 – 4 = x = –18. Therefore, Column B is equal to –18. The correct answer is A, since –10 is greater than –18.

28 **Answer: A**

   Explanation: Since the ratio of rabbits to squirrels is 2:3, there are two rabbits for every three squirrels. Let 2x represent the number of rabbits and then 3x represent the number of squirrels. So 2x + 3x = 225. Combine similar terms: 5x = 225. Divide both sides by 5: 5x ÷ 5 = 225 ÷ 5 = x = 45. The number of squirrels is 3x, so 3(45) = 135. The correct answer is A, since 135 is greater than 120.

29 **Answer: B**

   Explanation: Find the value in each of the columns. In Column A, multiply the number of ducks by the number of feet each duck has which is 2: 23 × 2 = 46. In Column B, multiply the number of cars by the number of wheels each car has which is 4: 15 × 4 = 60. Column B which is 60 is greater than Column A which is 46, so the correct answer is B.

30 **Answer: B**

   Explanation: Mean refers to the average of the numbers. To find the average, add all the given numbers and divide the sum by the number of items. In Column A, add the numbers in set A: 50 + 78 + 88 + 92 = 308. Divide by 4: 308 ÷ 4 = 77. Column A is 77. Then, median refers to the middle number in a list. There are four numbers in set B and since there is no middle number, get the two middle pair number. Add them and divide them by 2: (89 + 92) ÷ 2 = 181 ÷ 2 = 90.5. Column B is 90.5. The correct answer is B, since Column B is greater than Column A.

31 **Answer: C**

   Explanation: The sale price of the snowboard is $63. It is 70% of the original price. Let x be the original price. To find its original price, the equation is 0.70x = $63. Divide both sides of this equation by 0.70 to get x = $90. Column A is 90 $ which is equal to Column B, so the correct answer is C.

32 **Answer: A**

   Explanation: Column A contains the number of years in a century which is 100. Column B contains the number of years in a decade which is 10. The correct answer is A, since 100 is greater than 10.

33 **Answer: B**

   Explanation: Plug in a value for y, such as y is greater than 0. Let y be 8. Plug in the value in each expression and convert to decimal to compare. In Column A, $\frac{5}{y}$ is $\frac{5}{8}$ or 0.625. In Column B, $\frac{y}{9}$ is $\frac{8}{9}$ or 0.889. Column B is greater than Column A, so the correct answer is B.

34 **Answer: C**

   Explanation: The athletes and coaches together make 154 in total. Considering that each bus can hold 48 people, divide the total number of people by 48: 154 ÷ 48 = 3 r. 10. Therefore, four buses are needed. The two columns are equal, so the correct answer is C.

Grades 4–5   Practice Test 3 Session 2

35 **Answer: C**

Explanation: In Column A, to divide the fractions, you have to change the division sign to a multiplication sign and get the reciprocal of the second fraction: $\frac{6}{12} \times \frac{7}{2} = \frac{42}{24}$. To compare, convert it to a decimal: $\frac{42}{24} = 1.75$. Column A and Column B are equal, so the correct answer is C.

36 **Answer: B**

Explanation: To compare, write the given number word in a numeral form. In Column A, one hundred twenty-five thousandths is 0.125. Column B which is 125,000 is greater than 0.125, so the correct answer is B.

37 **Answer: B**

Explanation: In Column A, the even integers are 24, 16, 32, 12 and 34. Add them to get 118. In Column B, the odd integers are 45, 5, 73, 65 and 91. Add them to get 279. The correct answer is B, since 279 is greater than 118.

38 **Answer: B**

Explanation: To find the number of white marbles, get the two-fifths of 345. Remember that the word "of" means to multiply: $\frac{2}{5} \times 345 = \frac{690}{5} = 138$. Column A is 138. Column B which is 150 is greater than Column A which is 138; thus the correct answer is B.

39 **Answer: C**

Explanation: Plug in the value of z in each of the expressions in the column. In Column A, (34)(5z) = (34)[5(12)] = (34)(60) = 2,040. In Column B, (34z)(5) = [34(12)](5) = (408)(5) = 2,040. The two columns are equal, so the correct answer is C.

40 **Answer: C**

Explanation: Plug in a value for p. Let p be 8. In Column A, 8^2 can also be written out as 8 × 8 = 64. In Column B, -8^2 can also be written out as −8 × −8 = 64. The correct answer is C, because any positive or negative value plugged in to the expressions, the answer will always be equal.

41 **Answer: B**

Explanation: Column A contains the number of hours in a day which is 24. Column B contains the number of seconds in a minute which is 60. The correct answer is B, since 60 is greater than 24.

42 **Answer: A**

Explanation: Square both expressions to compare without the square roots. In Column A, $\left(5\sqrt{3r}\right)^2 = 25(3r) = 75r$. In Column B, $\left(3\sqrt{5r}\right)^2 = 9(5r) = 45r$. Since the value of r is a positive number, the correct answer is A, 75r is always greater than 45r.

43 **Answer: A**

Explanation: In Column A, divide 558 by 9 to get 62. The correct answer is A, since 62 is greater than 61.

44 **Answer: C**

Explanation: Column A contains the primes between 40 and 50 which are 41, 43 and 47. Column B contains the primes between 1 and 6 which are 2, 3 and 5. Each column is equal to 3, so the correct answer is C.

45 **Answer: C**

Explanation: Use the formula distance = rate × time. Gab's rate is 56 and his distance is 42: 42 = 56t. Solve the equation by dividing both sides by 56: $\frac{42}{56} = \frac{56t}{56} = 0.75 = t$. Therefore, Column A is 0.75 hours which is equivalent to 45 minutes. The two columns are equal, so the correct answer is C.

Grades 4–5	Practice Test 3 Session 2

46 **Answer: A**

   Explanation: In Column A subtract 678 from 123,456 to get 122,778. In Column B, subtract 786 from 123,456 to get 122,670. The correct answer is A, since 122,778 is greater than 122,670.

47 **Answer: A**

   Explanation: Find the value in each of the column. In Column A, you have to square 9 which means you have to multiply 9 by itself: $(9)^2 = 81$. In Column B, you have to find the square root of 121 which means the number that when you multiply by itself is equal to 121: $\sqrt{121} = 11$. Column A is greater than Column B, so the correct answer is A.

48 **Answer: C**

   Explanation: Find the total cost of the items in each of the column. In Column A, there are two notebooks and a bag: $2(\$1.5) + \$12 = \$3 + \$12 = \$15$. In Column B, there are bag, pad paper and a box of crayons: $\$12 + \$1 + \$2 = \$15$. Both columns are $15, so the correct answer is C.

49 **Answer: B**

   Explanation: In Column A, the number 1 to any power is 1 and 2^3 can be written out as $2 \times 2 \times 2$ is equal to 8. So Column A is $1 + 8$ is equal to 9. Column B which is 25 is greater than 9, so the correct answer is B.

50 **Answer: C**

   Explanation: Evaluate the given expression by subtracting 3 from both sides to get $5x = 15$. Now, divide both sides by 5: $\frac{5x}{5} = \frac{15}{5}$ to get $x = 3$. Both columns are equal to 3, so the correct answer is C.

51 **Answer: B**

   Explanation: Column A contains the circumference of the circle. The formula in finding the circumference of the circle is $C = 2\pi r$. Plug in the value of the radius: $2(3.14)(23 \text{ cm}) = (6.28)(23 \text{ cm}) = 144.44$ cm. To compare, make them similar units by converting the Column B to cm: $2 \text{ m} \times 100 = 200$ cm. The correct answer is B, because 200 cm is greater than 144.44 cm.

52 **Answer: B**

   Explanation: Evaluate the expression in Column A using PEMDAS. Work with the parentheses first: $\frac{3}{4}(12 + 48) - 25$: $\frac{3}{4}(60) - 25$. Multiply: $\frac{3}{4}(60) - 25 = 45 - 25$. Subtract: $45 - 25 = 20$. 30 is greater than 20, so the correct answer is B.

53 **Answer: C**

   Explanation: In Column A, three hundredths is also written as $\frac{3}{100}$. The two columns are equal, therefore the correct answer is C.

54 **Answer: A**

   Explanation: Write the quantities in their standard form. In Column A, $30,000 + 400 + 20 + 5 + 0.004$ is $30,425.004$. In Column B, $30,000 + 400 + 20 + 0.5 + 0.004$ is $30,420.504$. Column A is greater than Column B, so the correct answer is A.

55 **Answer: A**

   Explanation: Using slope-intercept ($y = mx + b$) form where m is the slope of the linear equation, the slope of the line in Column A is 2 and the slope of the line in Column B is $\frac{1}{2}$. 2 is greater than $\frac{1}{2}$, so Column A is the correct answer.